Sun of gOd

Sun of gOd

CONSCIOUSNESS AND THE SELF-ORGANIZING FORCE
THAT UNDERLIES EVERYTHING

by Gregory Sams

WEISERBOOKS
San Francisco, CA / Newburyport, MA

First published in 2009 by Red Wheel/Weiser, LLC
With offices at: 500 Third Street, Suite 230, San Francisco, CA 94107
www.redwheelweiser.com

ISBN: 978-1-57863-454-5

Library of Congress Cataloging-in-Publication Data is available upon request.

Cover and text design by Gopa & Ted2, Inc. • Typeset in Palatino LT 10/15.
Cover photograph © Sara Leigh Lewis.
Page 14 © Michael Bath, page 77 © Stephan Seip, page 86 © Fred Espenak, page 88 © NASA/SOHO, page 123 © Gregory Sams, page 136 © John Walsh, page 206 © Kenneth Libbrecht.

Printed in Canada
TCP

10 9 8 7 6 5 4 3 2 1

Table of Contents

Dedicated to my father and to my Sun

Foreword

FOR TENS of thousands of years our ancestors lived in intimate proximity to what they believed were spirit worlds inhabited by non-physical supernatural beings, with whom they communicated. They saw spirits in mountains and trees and thunderstorms. Ocean and sky were alive with spirit. Fire and earth were filled to the brim with it. Entities and intelligences existed out there, inherent and immanent in every possible combination of seen and unseen realms.

For about the last five thousand years various "religions" have claimed hegemony over the ways we approach these spirit realms and beings, often preferring to narrow down the focus to just one "god."

During the past three hundred years, and particularly in the last hundred years, a form of thinking has arisen—it calls itself science—which in some cases makes a virtue of refusing to investigate such matters at all and in others proclaims that there are no spirit worlds, and no non-physical supernatural beings, and actively derides those who continue to believe in such "myths."

In fact science has no evidence of the nonexistence of spirit worlds and non-physical supernatural beings and is wrong to allow us to think that it does. When a scientist asserts, for example, that there is no such thing as the soul and no possibility of life after death, he or she is not making a statement of fact based on empirical observations and repeatable experiments but rather a statement of unexamined prejudice based on personal beliefs about the nature of reality. True, the body in which the consciousness of the individual was previously enshrined has died, but the scientific/materialist proposal that consciousness cannot exist separately from the body—and thus has died with the body—is a metaphysical assumption, not an empirically demonstrated fact. The alternative proposition, which the world's wisest men and women have unanimously agreed upon for all but the last hundred years, is that on death our consciousness passes on in some way into another plane or dimension of existence.

Our best hope to gain knowledge of such mysteries is through the techniques that shamans in hunter-gatherer societies have developed, over tens of thousands of years, to contact the spirit world. In my opinion, no one, no matter how well-qualified as a scientist, should venture definitive conclusions concerning the nature of reality until they themselves have experienced shamanistic out-of-body journeys—and fortunately such voyages are now made possible by access to Ayahuasca, the vine of the shamans, and other consciousness-shifting plants.

I am no shaman, but my personal experiences with Ayahuasca have opened my eyes to the contrary possibility—namely that the fundamental unit of reality is not matter but the spirit that animates and organizes it, and that there may indeed be no dichotomy between spirit and matter because these realms are so thoroughly intertwined and promiscuously interconnected. The problem rather is one of perception—that the logical-positivist, empiricist bias of Western science has so conditioned us to focus on gross matter, as though there is nothing else, that we have become impervious to the subtler fields of spirit that interpenetrate and surround it.

Into this debate Gregory Sams has now stepped with the fertile thesis that he puts forward in his new book, *Sun of gOd*. Like many other good ideas, it is not so much new as newly and freshly stated in these pages, and cast against a new reference frame. Also like many other good ideas, it is essentially simple. What Gregory is proposing, in his own words, is that "a universal consciousness pervades all matter; whatever its form of existence—that this consciousness is the vibrational DNA of the universe." He then specifically asks us to consider the possibility that our Sun is "a living conscious being with an intelligence that dwarfs our own . . . Does it not seem unlikely that such an enabler and supporter of life [the Sun] would itself be just an inanimate unconscious accident of the cosmos?"

It is important to emphasize that Gregory is not merely suggesting "that Sun is a large complex system with some form of self-governing intelligence to it," but also that "it is a living being, aware of itself and its place in Universe . . . that its power of consciousness is so far beyond what we enjoy that it should be accorded deity status of a high order . . ."

I was reminded, when reading such passages in *Sun of gOd*, of hymns in the *Ancient Egyptian Book of the Dead* addressed to the Sun-god Ra, praising him as a great, seeing and hearing conscious being, charting a course across untold space for millions of years until his own hours came to an end.

There is great reverence for the Sun in the texts of the ancient Egyptians and clear evidence of a belief that it is a sentient spiritual being that has chosen to incarnate in the form of a radiant solar disk in order to bring light, life and love into a sea of darkness. Alas in modern society such reverence is nowhere to be found. The mainstream religions have stigmatized Sun-worship as paganism, mainstream science conditions us from birth to regard all matter, including the Sun, as ultimately "dead," and many people relate to it only as some sort of gigantic outdoor tanning lamp or possible source of cancers.

The Sun can look after itself and ultimately has no need of our worship. It does what it does regardless of our wishes or behavior. But unfortunately this is not true for the diverse ecosystems that once covered large parts of the earth and that human civilization seems hell-bent on destroying. Let us speak only of the enchanted wilderness of the Amazon rainforest destroyed to make space for soya-bean farms exploiting cheap labour to work land that will cease to be viable within a decade. In a world that reverenced spirit, the voices of the spirits of the jungle would long ago have been heard and a sane alternative to the present greedy madness would have been found.

It may already be too late for the Amazon, which has never stood in greater need of a few good friends, but to the extent it succeeds in restoring spirit to its proper place as the foundation and energizing principle of all life in Gregory Sams' new book, and new way of seeing, will have a part to play in the global change of consciousness that is now, as never before, so desperately needed.

Graham Hancock, 2008

Recalling the forgotten
now the box is open

PEOPLE MIGHT LOOK at you strangely if you tell them you believe that the Sun thinks and that it truly is a celestial being. Yet this was once the normal mindset wherever intelligent people inhabited the planet. This understanding appeared obvious at the time, though we now unthinkingly dismiss it as naïvely ignorant. We might think that science has taught us better, but it was not science that dismissed our notion of the Sun being a "being." It was the Christian church that prohibited such thoughts, banning and burning those who held them, including scientists and scholars. Their new god's child Jesus took the birthday and many other features of solar deities whose role his legend-makers usurped.

We will never know just how well-developed human knowledge and understanding were before the Christian era began. Bodies of work existed in libraries and universities containing centuries of the accumulated knowledge of scholars on subjects ranging from agriculture to architecture to astronomy. These distant predecessors of ours built the fabled Hanging Gardens of Babylon and the great pyramids of Egypt. Throughout the ages, great human minds applied themselves to the study of spirituality and the healing arts as well as to harder sciences such as metallurgy and chemistry.

Unfortunately, little of the accumulated knowledge of pre-Christian times survives. Zealous Christians from the fourth century onwards assiduously burned all the pagan literature they could find, at a time when books were painstakingly copied by hand, with copy locations known. They kept some records, of course, proudly detailing the documents tracked down for destruction, but often just torched the lot, as did a Christian mob in 391 at the Library of Alexandria, believed to have contained 700,000 documents. It had all been written by pagans. Was there a pyramid-building manual? We'll never know.

The Christians did not look kindly upon those choosing to retain pagan traditions recognizing the consciousness of our Sun, the goddess of the Earth or other unapproved god-like entities. Sun worship was considered far more heinous than killing, raping, or robbing. What little we know today of ancient traditions concerning the Sun is primarily derived from the notes of pious and biased chroniclers who made it their business to destroy all trace of that about which they wrote. But we can rediscover.

A powerful Church claimed the monopoly on spirituality and subsequently banned anything they thought to be in conflict with that monopoly. Alchemy, astrology, spiritualism, soothsaying, chanting, or dancing naked under the moon could get one into serious trouble. The last item still can. A patent was effectively put upon the ecstatic state, with punishment meted out to those caught seeking a religious experience by other than Church-approved means.

Centuries under the influence of organized religion have, perhaps, damaged our facility to understand the spirit that surrounds us. We readily accept that many of the invisible features of this existence are a very real part of our lives—things such as gravity, electricity, radio, air pressure, happiness, and the wind. Yet the most important invisible feature of our existence continues to be shrouded in mystery, misunderstanding, and often outright disbelief—though it is the one that enables us to experience all the rest. The invisible world of spirit, a world that science denies and religion mystifies, is perhaps more real and tangible than we ever have imagined.

We ourselves manifest life because of the spirit attached to our physical bodies. For humans, the belief that we share our world with other manifestations of spirit stretches beyond the roots of history to a time before we had learned how to make knives or bread, let alone atomic bombs and Pop-Tarts. Spirit was perceived in the planet itself and in the Sun that nurtures all upon it. In the thirty thousand years or so since we have taken human culture beyond the stone axe, it is only in the relatively recent past that our primal understanding of spirit has been directed into the twisted channels of organized religion, or extinguished altogether by science.

Today we have few means to feel or understand the common mindset that prevailed until relatively recently—the mindset that saw our world as a unified phenomenon and recognized the shared spirit in all its components. It was perfectly respectable that scientists from Aristotle through to Isaac Newton would study fields now shunned as occult practice. Most of the early astronomers were also astrologers, attributing spirit and personality to the Sun, moon and planets. The alchemist in Newton recognized the spirit in matter, devoting more attention and pages to the subject than he did to his world-changing *Principia Mathematica*. Perhaps Newton's unique ability to understand the mechanics of the physical world might have arisen from the greater time he spent in studying its spirit.

We can easily understand why science does not wish to accept the existence of spirit—of any consciousness existing outside our experience of it in a human body.

> *Where there is a duty to worship the sun it is pretty sure to be a crime to examine the laws of heat.*
> **—VOLTAIRE**

Acceptance opens the door to a veritable Pandora's box of quackery and hocus-pocus, things that science has "religiously" sought to exclude from its arena. But I am afraid that it is too late. The box is open.

Scientists have already discovered spirit and the evidence shouts at them from their own research.

Though some quantum physicists think openly of spirit and universal consciousness, most scientists still retain a strong bias against even considering the subject, let alone studying it. Ironically, the roots of this prejudice arise from a "tradition" initiated by church decree, supported more by habit than by the scientific method. It dates to a time when more than a reputation could get burned for straying into areas branded occult by a powerful church. A result of this is that dogmatic men wearing funny outfits have ever since enjoyed a virtual monopoly on the study of all things spiritual. Today the New Age has opened some nearly forgotten fields to study once again, but heaven help any scientist who takes a serious and open-minded look at it.

The nature of spirit is a big subject and it is a terrible shame that it has for so long been the exclusive preserve of organized religions. There would be little need for a book like this if such an artificial barrier had not been erected between science and spirit. I hope to at least make a small chip in that barrier.

In this book you will never be asked to believe something because the test tube proved it, or because some special spirit channelled it, or because somebody else said so—whatever their qualifications or titles. Believe anything only if it makes sense to you—and continues to do so in every situation of your life and from every angle you look at it. Do not take anything on board as an article of faith—or believe it just because it mixes in the company of wisdom, or is delivered with great enthusiasm or wit.

Let us not confuse the concept of having trust in the Universe with having blind faith in religious or scientific explanations of it. Keep an open mind as you travel these pages, but receive and reject whatever you like in the course of the journey. I reserve the right to change my own mind about anything herein as time goes by.

With due respect:
▸ It would be incorrect to capitalize god, when discussing different interpretations of the One. Therefore, to differentiate the concept

of a single or supreme god from the multiplicity of other gods out there, that One, however interpreted, will be referred to as gOd.

▶ There is one Universe, one Sun and one planet Earth. Why these named places are not capitalized in general usage is a mystery to me. These words are all capitalized.

▶ It is not usual with proper nouns such as Jupiter, Madrid or Arthur, to prefix them with "the," as in "the Jupiter." In these pages the terms Universe, Sun and Earth will not always be preceded by "the."

Do not believe in anything simply because you have heard it. Do not believe in anything simply because it is spoken and rumored by many. Do not believe in anything simply because it is found written in your religious books. Do not believe in anything merely on the authority of your teachers and elders. Do not believe in traditions because they have been handed down for many generations. But after observation and analysis, when you find that anything agrees with reason and is conducive to the good and benefit of one and all, then accept it and live up to it.

—BUDDHA

From nothing to now
maybe we just got lucky

"Science without religion is lame, religion without science is blind."
—ALBERT EINSTEIN, 1941

O NCE BEFORE a time there was nothing—so the story goes. No bugs, no planets, no stars—neither clouds of cosmic dust nor space for them to be within. Nothing for time to clock. And then came space, and with it substance, materializing as a soup of subatomic particles during the first moments of a newborn Universe. Endlessly recombined and rearranged, those original particles continue to make up all that's physical—from comets to custard pies, from our Sun to a swallow and the air in which it flies.

The scientific establishment takes pride in its efforts to explain Universe, from the Big Bang until recently, as a combination of chance events untouched by any intelligence or consciousness—until, of course, we human beings arrived upon the scene. The outlandish explanations of creation offered by organized religions serve to convince many that science must have the better answers. But the sometimes stranger theories of cosmologists explaining how dumb particles accidentally bumbled into becoming stars and fleshy organisms make many cling to the irrational ideas of organized religion, if only for tradition's sake. While the concept of a divine planner plotting planetary orbits and designing the DNA of each new species does not bear rational exploration, could the extraordinary route from then to now have been random process, devoid of any intent or consciousness?

That there was a beginning to the Universe is one point upon which science and religion do agree. Outside the religious arena, this singular moment came to be known as the Big Bang—a unique, naturally occurring random event, albeit one of literally cosmic proportions. Much of the Universe that we know is empty space but before the Big Bang there was not even that. This theoretical starting point, set at 13.7 billion years[1] ago, brought forth massive amounts of subatomic particles into a newly formed space. These individual particles soon assembled themselves into simple atoms of hydrogen and helium—the first recognizable matter in Universe.

Universe's original atoms, instead of dispersing like ink in a glass of water, grouped together into giant clouds of thin gas dotted about the newly formed cosmos. And if our Universe were seen as a being that was 100 years old, it would have been within its first few years[2] that these clouds of simple atoms began condensing into many denser balls of gas. Within a relative one to two hours the pressure in these balls became so intense that contained and steady nuclear reactions kicked off within the hearts of the newborn stars. Illumination came to the cosmos.

In our local galaxy, the Milky Way, we have a hundred billion or more stars. Four and a half billion years ago one of them, our own Sun, was born. Soon afterwards it collected nine balls of concentrated matter around it and, by chance, the third ball away had a hot center, a high water content and a thin atmosphere of gases surrounding it—gases that would be deadly to most life forms we know. Earth spent its first half billion or so years just chilling out and settling down to a quieter existence.

Before its first billion years passed, Earth had settled down enough for organic life to appear, as bacteria became its first living occupants. This incredibly versatile and persistent life form may have arisen upon Earth spontaneously. But it is so difficult to explain how bacteria could have evolved in the available time that it is easier for some cosmologists to adopt the panspermia principle and believe that the first bacteria came in on a comet, or by other means from outer space. Panspermia does not suggest how and where such a finely-crafted living device as the bacterium could have developed accidentally, just that it was probably somewhere else. However it came to be, this highly adaptable life force soon colonized the surface of planet Earth, as its waters and land mass became host to a growing array of increasingly complex microbial life forms.

The thin layer of soil that forms a patchy covering over the continents controls our own existence and that of every other animal of the land. Without the soil, land plants as we know could not grow, and without plants no animal could survive.
—RACHEL CARSON, *SILENT SPRING,* 1963

For about 3 billion years, single-celled microbes were all there was. These tiny organisms mutated and adapted as they nibbled away at the rocks and other inorganic matter of Earth, creating a living soil. Bacterial activity slowly altered the mixture of gases in the atmosphere and the organic content of the oceans, allowing more complex life forms to arise upon Earth. These more complex life forms, whether worms or human beings, provide a warm home for more bacteria than there are cells in their own bodies—many more. And this has all come into place, we are assured, without a drop of intention or intelligence, by randomly replicating dumb bacteria accidentally paving the way for more complex life forms—life forms in which they play a vital role.

These microscopic creatures bumped around and evolved, accidentally exchanging genes in the process and developing more complexity and adaptability to an environment that they were themselves gradually changing. That was all there was until about 550 million years ago, about 4 billion years into the planet's 4.5 billion-year history. This was when more complex life began to appear in the waters of the planet, as single-celled organisms started to join together into the first soft-bodied symbiotic multi-celled organisms. Things like jellyfish started appearing in the fossil records.

From jellyfish onwards, we begin seeing the first records of creatures that we can identify with: living things that have external, as well as internal, structure; organisms that can see and move around; creatures with sexual appetites and territorial tendencies. Organic life continued to evolve as larger, more complex multi-celled creatures appeared in the planet's waters.

Darwinists tell us that this developing life arose from purely random and accidental genetic selection. The fossil records illustrate Darwin's discovery of the gradual changes to a species accomplished over millions of years of adaptation to a changing environment. There doesn't need to be a big, bearded geezer "up there" who designed the bee, the oak tree, and our ancestors, the apes. But it is purely an assumption that the entire process of evolution is accidental and without intent, an assumption that was not made by Darwin himself. While fossil records chart the gradual steps of evolutionary change, they shed no light upon the origin of genetic novelty.

The fossils show that from around 400 million years ago some of these water-living creatures worked out how to spend more time out of water, eventually learning how to obtain their oxygen directly from the air, a novel concept at the time. A drying environment drove the change in many cases as did the quest for food. Perhaps even curiosity played a part. Fungi and plants successfully moved from the oceans to land during the same period and began adjusting to the new conditions.

Eventually, through evolution, cooperation, competition, natural selection, and adaptation, ever-increasing varieties of animals developed, from the tiny to the massive. The giant dinosaurs seemed to do best of these land-based creatures and appeared to rule the world for 150 million years or so.

About 65 million years ago, during the era of the dinosaurs, a new design style arrived in the form of smaller, softer animals: mammals. Small players on the world scene, this group shared a large range of common biological and emotional features. A comet hitting the earth is believed to have triggered the demise of the dinosaur, enabling mammals to thrive and diversify. These mammals soon branched into many new forms, including the primates.

If Earth were 100 years old, then it would have been a little over 2 weeks ago that something unusual happened. In fact, it was 5 million years ago that some of these primates evolved to the point where they spent a lot of time upright and eventually mastered the two-foot balancing act.

One week ago in a century-old planet, something really remarkable occurred. The brains of these upright hominids started to become larger as they used them to outwit or escape stronger and faster competitors. They made stone axes and cooked with fire. The first *Homo sapiens* had arrived and at some point, soon after, they found time to reflect on life and become aware of their own existence, passing knowledge from generation to generation.

Apparently it is at this fuzzy point that consciousness and intelligence arise in this vast 13.7-billion-year-old Universe. Yes, we are here and we know it and we've got enough brains to plan things and produce stuff. But until our arrival, everything that had happened to date was driven by the happenstance of unintentional unintelligent accident. Of course scientists now accept as possible that some other conscious intelligent beings, kind of like us, might have developed a little earlier in another stellar system.

Up to this point, according to scientific tradition, all other life forms on this planet simply made genetically programmed responses to external stimuli. They had no freedom of choice and were no more aware of their own existence than is a rock. Except, some argue, for orangutans and a handful of other mammals who realize that they are what they see in a mirror—like we do.

Yes, from the Big Bang onwards, it might have all been just one fantastic cosmic accident—an accident that has blessed us with our existence, and left us with the time and intellect to ponder questions like this about the nature of it all. This is how the standard textbooks would have us view it—a random sequence of events, cosmic and mundane, eventually and unintentionally conspiring to create the conditions for our existence and that of other life forms.

One of the reasons that scientists for so long discounted the possibility of intelligent life in outer space is the incredibly unlikely chain of circumstance and co-incidence that enabled it to manifest on Earth. Life obviously did happen—we are here to witness it—but the possibility of it happening somewhere else in the Universe, accidentally, is about as likely as one of us winning the lottery every day for a month. Scientifically possible, of course, but unlikely to happen more than once in a purely chance-driven Universe.

Could Universe have just been one ongoing accidental progression leading from nothing to everything? The alternative is to consider that consciousness, however primitive, was involved in the unfolding of the cosmos, or was instigated somehow by the cosmos itself. It could be that consciousness existed before the Big Bang, but how can we speculate upon a period before time in a place without space? It does, though, seem just a little arrogant to believe that our Universe waited for 13.698 billion years, until we came along, to manifest the phenomenon of consciousness—and to assume that ours is the only type of vessel able to experience it.

Homo sapiens did not appear on the earth, just a geologic second ago, because evolutionary theory predicts such an outcome based on themes of progress and increasing neural complexity. Humans arose, rather, as a fortuitous and contingent outcome of thousands of linked events, any one of which could have occurred differently and sent history on an alternative pathway that would not have led to consciousness.

—**STEPHEN J. GOULD,** *SCIENTIFIC AMERICAN,* OCTOBER 1994

What is this?
we'd not be here without it

WHEN OUR BODIES move and our brains think, we are experiencing the effect of there being consciousness in residence. For all its miraculous wonders, our body is just a lump of meat without consciousness. Can it be that consciousness spontaneously arrives as a result of getting the correct assembly of ears, eyes, nerves, muscles, skin, and so forth together? Or could it be that these are simply the tools through which our personal consciousness experiences and affects the world that we inhabit?

Consciousness, the power behind our mind and being, is essentially an invisible phenomenon. Though it follows us most places, we cannot see or physically locate it—but just try living without it. As with the wind rushing through the trees, what we experience are the effects of consciousness.

So just what is this stuff that we are forever talking about raising or lowering? What is this quality that distinguishes our complex body with being alive and vital?

What is *this?*

There is no accepted standard definition for consciousness. Mystics and philosophers have devoted entire books to it, or summed it up with the two words: consciousness is. *Collins Millennium Dictionary,* rather unhelpfully, relegates consciousness to the end of its definition for conscious, as the noun version of the adjective—the thing that exists when we are not asleep or unconscious.

The Oxford English Dictionary is more comprehensive on consciousness, giving us six different definitions. These are:

1. Joint or mutual knowledge.

2. Internal knowledge or conviction, especially of one's ignorance, guilt, deficiencies, and so forth.

3. The fact or state of being conscious or aware of anything.

4. The state or faculty of being conscious as a condition or concomitant of all thought, feeling, and volition.

5. The totality of the impressions, thoughts and feelings that make up a person's conscious being.

6. The state of being conscious regarded as the normal condition of healthy waking life.

Confused? I'm not surprised. Consciousness is a tricky word to define—right up there with "God" and "infinity." The Latin roots of the word simply mean "with knowing," which is a basic prerequisite and foundation for each of the above six definitions. At its broadest and most basic, this "with knowing" is manifested by a simple awareness of being. If a frog is aware of whatever "frogness" is like, then it is conscious of its existence and thus deemed a vessel of consciousness. This will be the simple definition which I use: **consciousness = with knowing.**

We will not get a lot of help with describing consciousness from scientists. It often seems as though they conscientiously try to sidestep the subject as much as possible. The principles of science hamper the study of subjects for which there are no means of detection, quantification, or categorization. Neither can scientists reliably reproduce experimental findings about consciousness, nor comfortably follow in the tradition of many earlier researchers into the subject. That many of those researchers were burned for their efforts, literally or figuratively, has been an effective deterrent to later generations.

Until quite recently, for those scientists who believe humans to be conscious, it has been assumed that no other animals shared the facility—in the sense of being aware of its own existence. Some scientists make a case for porpoises, baboons, or orangutans because they can be seen playing for no apparent purpose other than to have fun, or are able to recognize themselves in mirrors. But otherwise the curtains came down on all other life forms, which are believed to be following programmed survival-driven behavior with no consciousness, reason or free will involved in the process.

Apparently because dogs don't recognize themselves in a mirror, they have no concept of their own selves even though they spend much of their life sniffing around in order to recognize the presence of other, different selves. This may seem as curious to many readers as it does to this writer, but at the time of writing, this prevailing mindset[3] is only beginning to be challenged. That this is the attitude taught when those in the establishment went to school is demonstrated by the need for *New Scientist* magazine, in 2005, to devote a cover story to controversial experiments intended to demonstrate the existence of self-awareness in animals.

Perhaps because scientists cannot detect and measure this subtle field, they are unable to demonstrate that anything other than us harbors consciousness. In the tradition of science, something cannot be considered to exist until it is possible to reliably prove or demonstrate that it does. This has traditionally left a lot out of their equations.

Many scientists and scholars have even convinced themselves that the human perception of consciousness is simply a "grand illusion" created by the physical activity of the brain. In contrast, most mystics, philosophers and ordinary people see consciousness as something definitive, and distinct from the physical body. Beyond our brain cells, past their firing neurons and all our senses, it seems like there is something else going on—some space or field in which our consciousness resides that is neither a physical component of our bodies, nor an illusion of our brains.

But how can we describe the parameters of a conscious mind—the borders or extent of it? Perhaps there is but one universal field of consciousness, and what we perceive as our own is simply the unique interface that our mind and personal spirit have with it. We could all be individual tenants renting space in a universal field where there is nothing to pay, in which we can occupy as much or as little space as we are capable of. We can at times expand our consciousness to embrace the infinite Universe, or live a small-minded life focused entirely upon the props surrounding our physical existence.

It may be beyond our highly developed intellect to tackle that most difficult of questions: Where does our consciousness come from and what happens to it when this physical shell expires? We might as well be individual molecules of water in a mountain lake trying to assess whether there is life after vapor, or contemplating what existence was like as ice or rain: "Yeah, man, I was the Amazon in a previous incarnation."

The science that is able to detect the faintest trace of any chemical in virtually anything cannot yet tell us if consciousness exists in the same room. The doctor still looks no farther than a lack of heartbeat or "brainstem death" to declare life's end. But these are just physical symptoms and no absolute guarantee that consciousness has departed. There are cases of recovered coma victims who were aware of everything happening around them, but whose conscious state was undetected by the doctors. Science knows more about the moon than it does about consciousness—and has certainly devoted more time and money to studying it.

Though we can sometimes "feel" somebody looking at us before we see them, why are there so few tools that are able to detect and calibrate this all-important consciousness? Is it because this was for so long thought to be a fruitless area of scientific endeavor better left to the church—or is there another reason? Perhaps it is because we live within a consciousness-saturated Universe that we find it a challenge to define or detect the item itself. Perhaps it is the very ubiquitous all-infusing nature of consciousness that makes it so difficult to identify or measure.

All-infusing consciousness is by no means a new idea. This is what Korean, Chinese, and Japanese cultures have long recognized as *Chi*— life-force energy that is everywhere at all times, and accessible to the properly tuned mind. Tuning into and understanding this universal energy field is central to Far Eastern schools of medicine, meditation, exercise, and martial arts such as Tai Chi and Chi Kung. Whether deep in a cave or high in a plane, it is always there.

In India, the term *Prana* describes the same life-force energy, sometimes described as the divine breath of the Universe. An understanding and channelling of Prana is vital to all forms of yoga, and basic to any practitioner of Hinduism. It is considered the primary energy of the Universe, without which nothing else could exist. The Greeks recognized an intelligence, which they called Mind, that infused all nature and brought it intelligence and form. The Maya described something similar with the term Ik. Wilhelm Reich, in the 20th century, called it orgone energy and created devices designed to focus and channel it. He died in prison in 1957, a year after the Food and Drug Administration banned and burned his books. The Great Sioux Nation of North America recognized Wakan-Tanka, a universal energy perceived by them as the Great Mystery and source of all power.

The phenomenon known as the Holy Spirit or Holy Ghost would appear to be the Christian equivalent of this universal field of spirit. The Holy Spirit is considered by Christianity to be a life force—the energy of gOd that is at work in our world. More recent church doctrine has relatively little to say about the nature of this third of the Holy Trinity. I found a curious explanation on a Christian website: "There's a practical reason for this: the Spirit is so hard to describe, that thinking about the Spirit too much will drive you loony. Virtually every description of the person Christians call the Holy Spirit finds itself at some point on the edge of the cliff of heresy (teaching lies about God)."[4] Surely that says something in itself. Islam avoids this confusing pitfall by expressly denying the Holy Spirit of the Christian Trinity.

Whatever it is named, the divine spirit is always perceived to be something with which our consciousness is fundamentally intertwined, whether we act in that knowledge or not. Religions of the East and philosophers through the ages have expressed the ultimate truth that "All is One." If there is sense to this then it is likely to be an ultimate unity of consciousness and not simply a manifestation on the physical plane. We cannot be expected to believe that the reference in the Book of Genesis to mankind being made in the "image of God" is referring to physical appearance—gOd looking just like us but a whole lot bigger, with a long white beard and flowing robes. Will He be sitting, or standing?

Historically, humans have long believed in forms of consciousness other than that which we experience in this physical body. For tens of thousands of years, the human species consistently believed in the existence of various forms of invisible spirits and entities—even categorizing them as angels, demons, fairies, ghosts, poltergeists, elves or other spirits, up to and including gOd.

Other special spirits were also recognized within the physical world, believed to inhabit great trees, seasonal winds, rivers, mountains, planets and so forth. In the wake of the Old Testament religions, we have become convinced that countless generations of our culturally developed ancestors were deluded by their superstitious senses. Today it is the scientists who assure us that such thoughts are nonsense, when once religious zealots would have burned us for thinking them.

The brilliant insights of scientists, and the benefits to all our lives achieved though the dedication of well-educated professionals applying the scientific method, will never be in question. But the pillar that is science in our society loses neither stature nor credibility by letting go of a taboo initially imposed by a ruling Church. There is something "out there" and there is no scientific reason why every scientist who strays, even accidentally, into areas once branded "occult" should continue to be ridiculed, decried, and denied. We will expand later upon how, in 1988, eminent French immunologist Jacques Benveniste stumbled across a memory in water that smacked of homeopathy—and upon the dire consequences to his career.

Over the millennia, countless thousands of physical people have borne witness to their own encounters with consciousness in a non-physical realm. In Graham Hancock's book, *Supernatural: Meetings with the Ancient Teachers of Mankind*, there are references to thousands of experiential accounts of encounters with "not of this world" beings that have taken place throughout history and across the globe. The author brings to our attention striking similarities in the detailed accounts of these first-hand experiences—similarities that crossed continents and centuries. The interpretation of such encounters may vary depending upon the personality and cultural background of the witness, and it is undeniably difficult to reproduce such experiences under laboratory conditions. But there is no sound scientific reason to dismiss many thousands of documented first-hand accounts of encounters—relegating each and every one of them to over-imagination, hallucination, clever trickery, or some other explainable delusion.

The whole drift of my education goes to persuade me that the world of our present consciousness is only one out of many worlds of consciousness that exist.
—WILLIAM JAMES, AMERICAN PHILOSOPHER, 1842-1910

Our long-standing belief in non-physical, and usually invisible, entities must have been well established at the onset of organized religions. There would have been nothing for religious zealots to organize were they not able to harness and channel, into their own chosen brand, the strength of our intuitive belief in the existence of an invisible Other.

This belief in non-material entities, so ingrained for millennia, indicates that what could be described as our "natural mindset" has no requirement for consciousness to inhabit a breathing, organic, physical body. If we can accept the existence of a non-physical consciousness, then we can have no fundamental objection to considering the existence of consciousness in objects we now view as completely inanimate—devoid of being or awareness. Some of this inanimate "stuff" manages to display quite organized and strangely intelligent behavior.

Simply because we human beings pick up our perception of the world around us through the tools at hand, it does not follow that they are therefore the only tools through which the world may be experienced. We can hardly guess at what other vessels consciousness might inhabit, complex or simple. For all we know, the tree might be tickled by the ripple of a breeze; the volcano excited by its own eruption;

the thundercloud proud of its lightning; the mountain sublime in its majesty.

MICHAEL BATH

Volcanoes, mountains, oceans and other phenomena were regarded by ancient mankind as possessing accessible cognitive consciousness—though probably not as we know it. A worshipful respect for trees, particularly the oak, was extensive throughout most of Europe before Christianity arrived. Across the globe, specific trees were often singled out for special respect, forming the focus of sacred activity.

It was a widespread practice throughout the world to assign a spiritual personality to geological constructs such as mountains, rivers, and natural springs; and to meteorological phenomena such as seasonal winds, thunderclouds, and hurricanes. Were our human ancestors being deluded and misguided for those tens of thousands of years, or were they just following gut instincts—instincts that have been lost to us in a culture that finds factory-made baby formula preferable to mother's milk?

Is there some specific point at which a rock becomes a boulder, or a hill becomes a mountain? You will see, as we progress, that it becomes difficult to draw a fixed line between a mountain and a rock, an ancient oak and a blade of grass, a horse and a horsefly. The primary basis for considering consciousness to be unique to humanity is that we define it precisely by our own experience of it.

I am part of the sun as my eye is part of me,
that I am part of the earth my feet know perfectly
and my blood is part of the sea.
—D.H. LAWRENCE

Many who have closely studied orangutans and dolphins are convinced that these species display all the requisites of consciousness, and are aware of their individual selves. Let us imagine that we do extend the "official" boundary of consciousness beyond human beings—to orangutans and dolphins and a few other higher mammals such as whales and chimpanzees. Should this happen, there will inevitably be many who press for membership to be extended to gorillas, dogs, horses, and cats. Pigs are known to be very smart, too, and now we've got those clever tool-making New Caledonian Crows to consider.

Once the boundaries of consciousness are officially extended beyond human beings, the doors to the zoo will be truly open. It will soon become a difficult, if not impossible, endeavor for the philosopher or biologist to decide upon the dividing line between one higher mammal or bird and the next one down the line, below which no other animal enjoys consciousness. Will one breed of dog squeeze in and another not? Might rats be included but not mice? For all we know, crickets, worms, bacteria, and even plants might ultimately make it into the club—and then where would we be?

I have no problem with having no fixed line, since it is my belief (though no new idea) that a universal consciousness pervades all matter, whatever its form of existence—that this consciousness is the vibrational

DNA of the Universe. This is not to suggest that blades of grass are very clever or rocks all that sentient or that, individually, either play much of a part in the scheme of things. But perhaps even a grain of sand might know of its existence as a micro-part of the beach or desert—a life being polished and rearranged by the waves of water and wind?

This book never really leaves the subject of consciousness. It is a fascinating, elusive, and large subject. So let us leave small grains of sand for now, and take a look at other and higher extremes in the bandwidth of consciousness.

One, many, or both?
a question of divinities

HUMANS THROUGH the ages have given god or goddess status to anything perceived as containing considerably greater consciousness, spirit, and life-force than themselves. Something with powers and abilities beyond anything we can aspire to, fulfilling needs and objectives that we can hardly imagine—this has always been the stuff of gods.

The prevailing culture of the West has rarely viewed things like oceans or thunderclouds or mountains as being anything other than randomly reacting inanimate matter. Though it might be hard for us to understand, we can appreciate why it seemed apparent to earlier cultures that an element of consciousness was at play in these complex phenomena. Without science to explain it for them, they assumed that some form of conscious spirit must accompany such a structured and influential thing as an ocean or the Sun. And when that spirit, wherever it appeared, was judged to wield more lasting power and influence in the world than did the average human being, it was often accorded god status.

It was probably later in the development of religious thought that concepts such as love, agriculture and war were endowed with "gods of" status. In these instances it appears that simply by warrant of enough people focusing their consciousness upon a representative of common human experience, such a representation can assume the status of a deity. But this is only my guesswork. There are many well-researched works tracing the evolution of individual gods through different cultures, as their names and characteristics shift with different waves of emigration and conquest, amalgamation and adaptation. It is not surprising that there eventually arose those who viewed all this as a quite unholy mess.

There are fewer gods about today, arising in part from the historical imposition of "only-one-godism" upon much of the world by the monotheistic and militaristic Christian and Islamic religions. The principle of a judgemental universal deity delivering divine instruction through His prophets is still deeply embedded in our culture and law, even though church attendance may no longer be mandatory, nor sex in unapproved orifices an imprisonable offence. After experiencing almost 1,600 years of domination by organized religion in Western Europe, regular church attendance has plummeted to between two and twenty percent of the population in most European countries, including Britain, Germany, France, Switzerland, and the Scandinavian nations.

The shift away from the directed worship of organized religion is perhaps being offset by a substantial increase in those who worship a growing array of celebrity figures. The media, sports, and entertainment industries constantly create celebrities to satisfy humanity's seemingly insatiable urge to adulate. Film stars who are adored throughout the world achieve their almost godlike status by pretending to be other people. As Woody Allen once pointed out, most of us would be committed to mental institutions for similar behavior. Though the personal consciousness of media stars may be no greater than average, their near-god status probably arises from the amount of consciousness focused upon them. But the terminology "god" is seldom used to describe human celebrities. Instead we most commonly use the term star, an interesting choice of word.

A man is not as big as his belief in himself;
he is as big as the number of persons who believe in him.
—WOODROW WILSON, U.S. PRESIDENT

Dictionaries have no trouble with handling both multiple and single gods. The non-capitalized "god" defined by *Collins English Dictionary* is:

1. A supernatural being, who is worshipped as the controller of some part of the universe or some aspect of life in the world or is the personification of some force.

2. An image, idol, or symbolic representation of such a deity.

3. Any person or thing to which excessive attention is given.

There is quite obviously a lot of scope in this definition. In fact, some early Hindu sages put the official count at three hundred and thirty million gods.

Collins has only one definition for a capitalized God:

1. The sole Supreme Being, eternal, spiritual, and transcendent, who is the Creator and ruler of all and is infinite in all attributes.

In all seriousness, we must now ask just which Supreme Being is being referred to? How Supreme can this Being realistically be? In a Universe characterized by massive variations in scale and proportion, just how "infinite in all attributes" do we mean?

Though we know that our local Sun did not create the known Universe, and will someday die, it is easy to see how it was once a candidate for gOd as the sustainer of life on our planet. Everything in our lives, other than the stars twinkling in the night sky, is dependent upon Sun for it existence. Before we discovered that stars have births and deaths, the life span of Sun must have seemed as eternal to us as ours would seem to a mayfly. It certainly has organization and process going on, but is a fairly minor player in a cosmos filled with billions of galaxies, each crammed with billions of other stars. Most astronomers today would agree with Britain's Astronomer Royal Martin Rees, who believes that a small insect enjoys more complexity and, presumably, intelligence than does our Sun and other stars.

The next jump in scale that we might logically take, on the route to a Supreme Being, is to the galaxy that created the birth conditions for Sun and its neighbors in this nook of the Universe. What could be going on in the mind of a galaxy, if it has such a faculty? Before more powerful telescopes allowed us to look even farther, we thought our own galaxy to be the entire Universe. But now we know the Milky Way to be but one of billions of galaxies; it is difficult to view it as supreme or infinite, whether it has a mind or not.

Any candidate meeting the dictionary's demand of "infinite in all attributes" would have to embrace the entire Universe, whether such candidate was made of matter, spirit, or both. This would certainly be as far up the scale as we could travel when looking for a supreme gOd. There might be some other entity out there, visible or invisible, creating Universes as its function, or just for fun, but the concept does not invite sensible conjecture.

The idea of a gOd who looks after this infinite Universe sits uncomfortably with the singular gOd embraced by today's monotheistic religions. The gOd they have always worshipped is assumed to be devoting most of His attention to us and this little planet. He had made and crafted Earth, the Garden of Eden, Heaven, Hell, and the sky above, complete with stars—all for His beloved humanity to enjoy. This is a difficult character to reconcile with a creator of the Universe. In light of what we now know about the scale of this Universe, it would seem evident that any entity responsible for it remains essentially unrecognized by Christianity, Judaism, or Islam.

Once we get away from the big three monotheistic religions, the field opens up to a huge selection of gods and spirit characters. There was once extensive recognition of both visible and invisible entities that were considered to affect our lives while existing outside of our own mode of existence. Our ancestors sought to communicate with them for assistance in many areas of life, from success in conflict to the fertility of the soil and that of human beings. Early cultures considered spirit to be very real, though a supernatural phenomenon that was above and beyond the natural physical world that they experienced.

Sufficiently big spirits acquired the staus of gods, and it became common to recognize gods representing the spirit of agriculture, oceans, the arts, lightning, and so on.[5] Certain gods or spirits were considered preferable for specific options or peoples. A farmer was unlikely to request rain from the same spirit that his wife seeks help from in conceiving a healthy child.

Within those religions preaching worship of only one gOd we find that, in reality, their flocks choose from a larger selection of worship material than one would imagine. They do this through the medium of characters who are given a status that would, in earlier religions, have been reserved for lesser gods. These characters include Jesus and His mother, Mohammed, a legion of angels, as well as prophets, saints, and even their tombs. Choice of these will vary according to personal needs and preferences, as shepherds, sailors, lovers, and tailors each pray to their own patron saint or other form of spirit entity, serving the same function as did the diverse gods of older pagan religions.

All the members of the solar system, especially Sun, Earth, and its moon are regarded as gods by many early, and some current, religions. Each of the heavenly bodies is imbued with characteristics and attributes which are thought to have an influence upon our lives. Some might feel affinities with particular planets and the characters that are associated with them. It is intriguing that early peoples realized these steady lights in the sky to be so different to the twinkling stars, and that different cultures often ascribed similar characters and personalities to the planets.

The great divider between traditional and monotheist religions was disagreement over whether the god word refers to a singular gOd or to a multitude of gods. Yet why cannot it be possible for them to exist together—for there to be a multitude of gods, existing within the framework of a universal gOd embracing all? The assertion that there is only one gOd and that He, She, or It is the supreme and *only* god in existence comes linked to an arrogant assumption. This is that there are no entities possessing much more consciousness potential than human beings (including their angelic and saintly disembodiments) until we get up to that one big gOd, who runs the whole deal.

Those who believe in only one gOd are, then, praying directly to the greater gOd who fashioned this Universe out of clouds of thin gas—a gOd to the stars and the galaxies themselves. To this Universal Intelligence our tiny solar system, let alone the affection of our sweetheart, is unlikely to be a subject of any particular concern as long as it does not affect how Milky Way gets along with Andromeda and other neighboring galaxies. Gazing into the night sky we can pray to Her or Him as well and perhaps our electromagnetic impulses will still strike a cosmic chord in the bizarre infinity of the One. But it might be wise to reserve such direct requests for issues that are *really* important.

How great, how knowing?
less than we are told, more than we believe

"How can I believe in God when just last week I got my tongue caught in the roller of an electric typewriter?"—**WOODY ALLEN**

MANY STILL MAINTAIN their belief in a supreme gOd who is all-powerful and male. Yet however powerful one imagines such a gOd to be, relative to our own humble existence, it is without foundation to believe that such a character could have the power to accomplish everything He desires. For a start, He could give us a bit more harmony on Earth by having conversations with a few more prophets, and by saying the same things to them each time.

Don't we just wish that an all-powerful gOd could stop that horrific fire from sweeping through a joyous wedding party, or save the bus full of innocent children from plunging into a ravine? Could He not smite down some of those more heinous examples of the human race before they wreak horror upon their neighbors' children—or indeed whole civilizations, sometimes in His name? Perhaps even a most almighty gOd, if such exists, is still bound by the known laws and principles of the Universe—and perhaps some unknown ones, too.

Since the major monotheistic religions can accept the existence of only one gOd, then that god must embrace the entire Universe within His job description. With a range of responsibility like that, it is hard to imagine that there would be much attention to detail on this smaller satellite of Sun, one of hundreds of billions of stars in one of countless billions of galaxies. Our entire complex world is but a speck of dust in the vastness of the Universe, and we ourselves mere newcomers upon that speck of dust.

Whoever or Whatever makes all this possible is most certainly due our undying gratitude. But to consider that there exists a supreme being with full deterministic control of every single little thing going on within His realm is just plain silly, though somehow implied by the term Kingdom of gOd.

We are provided with life itself, and the capacity to develop uniquely human skills and traits. We live on a planet that supplies everything we need to feed, clothe, shelter, and amuse ourselves. We are able to love and to hate; to speak the truth and to lie; to imagine and to pretend. And we are able to make choices at every moment and every stage of our lives—choices that direct both our own destiny and that of all those who share our experience. This is the destiny that we ourselves create, using the gifts we are given.

Perhaps there is a gOd out there with preferences who tries to subtly steer or support our choices from time to time, sometimes with success and sometimes clearly not. But this is hardly all-powerful, however powerful it might be in comparison to our species. If gOd is omniscient, knowing everything that is going to happen, then how can He also be omnipotent and change what He knows is going to happen? It's an old conundrum.

One would expect any supreme-being type of gOd to know things and think on levels beyond our comprehension, bringing powers to bear that are beyond our imagination. But can all-knowingness be one of gOd's job skills, as so many devotees claim? It seems unlikely that within the great knowingness of such a being, He, She, or It would have conceived or anticipated the advent of the railway, or the many means by which we would one day store data on a small plastic disk. Did the good Lord look at those early catapults, lean back stroking His beard, and realize that eventually this sort of technology would lead to airplanes, geostationary communications satellites, and cell phone technology? I don't think so.

It wouldn't be much fun anyway, knowing everything that was going to happen because you had predetermined it. What's the point?

We are subject to natural laws, whether they are the uncontrollable ones triggering earthquakes and hurricanes, the predictable ones of gravity and chemistry, or the more inscrutable ones of synchronicity and karma. Through the agency of these last two, many believe that as individuals, as communities, as nations, and as the human species, we will reap what we sow—though the harvest may not always be distributed according to our standards of individual fairness.

The bottom line is that gOd and Its agents and allies, whichever ones we choose, have somehow brought about a world in which reward and retribution are integral working parts of the game. It is a world in which survival and growth is better assured by cooperation than by attack. The greatest reward in life is undoubtedly happiness and self-fulfilment, something which still eludes many, regardless of their political power, social status, or material wealth.

We do not require anybody to go around with a set of scales and a bagful of thunderbolts in order to calculate the good and the bad of our every action and then punish and reward us accordingly. That is already built into the program of being a social animal—a human being.

Our place in the firmament
Galileo tried to point it out

MOST OF US now recognize that planet Earth is circling a star called Sun, which is one of hundreds of billions of stars in our own large galaxy, the Milky Way. We take this for granted even though few of us can identify much in the night sky, or give much thought to the subject—unless we are astronomers or astrologers. Yet it is by no means obvious.

Many early thinkers and scientists, including the eminent Aristotle, were convinced that our Sun, the planets, and every object in the night sky revolved around Earth. Though erroneous, this geocentric viewpoint is clearly what it looks like from our perspective. A rotating Earth was thought to be impossible for many reasons, not least of which was the assumption that our atmosphere would be swept away in the process. This geocentric viewpoint, wherever it existed, would have had a profound effect upon religious thought.

The main monotheistic churches of the day felt safe in assuring their flocks that all this had been put here for their sole benefit. Humans were the focal point of this Universe, and thus obviously the most important object within it.⁶ It made sense that a universal gOd had put all this together for the benefit of life on planet Earth, specifically human life. The stars served as little more than decoration in the night sky. This assumption of centrality is fundamental to many of the church's most deeply held beliefs. Yet the premise that human life on Earth is the prime purpose of this Universal gOd's creation becomes less and less credible the further we look through the telescope.

In the early 16th century, without the aid of a telescope, Nicolas Copernicus came to the conclusion that Earth circled Sun once a year and that as it was making that journey it rotated around its own axis once every day. He believed that our Sun, not the Earth, was positioned at the center of the Universe. His radical and unproven theory, a big leap in the right direction, remained unpublished until shortly before his death in 1543. This inspired astronomer could never have anticipated the trouble he would subsequently cause the church, his employers at the cathedral in Frauenburg, Germany.

Five years after Copernicus died, Giordano Bruno was born in a small Italian town near Mt. Vesuvius. He rebelled against the monastic education imposed on him at a young age and managed to read a copy of Copernicus' dangerous book while still a teenager. He did not fit in a monastery and fled the cloisters at the age of 28 in fear of the Inquisition, believing he had glimpsed great truths that conflicted with Church dogma. He travelled to Geneva, France, and England, describing for the first time a Universe that was infinite and filled with other self-illuminated stars, akin to our Sun, surrounded by orbiting planets. He dared to question Aristotelian thinking and Church dogma about the virgin birth, the existence of Hell, and the infallible wisdom of Jesus. He was received by Queen Elizabeth but was thrown out of Oxford by its offended professors.

The Vatican was deeply concerned about Bruno's activities and in 1592 a young nobleman, and probable agent of the Inquisition, lured him back to Italy by feigning interest in publishing his work. One week later Bruno stood in court accused, and patiently explaining the basis and extent of his theories, refusing to retract them. He then withstood eight weeks of torture before being locked away in a dingy Roman dungeon for seven years. He then refused another offer to recant, leaving the Church no alternative but to burn him at the stake—the Christian method of execution that avoided shedding of blood. His tongue was tightly bound before he was burned lest, in his last moments alive, he should try to spread his dangerous ideas to the gathered crowd.

"Perhaps you, my judges, pronounce this sentence against me with greater fear than I who receive it."
—BRUNO, ON BEING SENTENCED

Twenty-three years after the church burned Bruno, Galileo Galilei peered through the newly invented telescope and began to put forward his conclusions regarding planetary orbits—the heliocentric versus the geocentric viewpoint. He gained great respect for his ideas, but was soon taken to task by the Inquisition—and charged with the crime of disseminating false knowledge. Offered the alternative of the death penalty, he agreed to recant and denounce his theory that Earth and all the other planets rotated around Sun. He was more lightly punished than was Bruno, with a lifetime of house arrest. Nearly four hundred years later, in 1992, the Vatican officially pardoned Galileo for his "crime." They finally forgave him his trespass.

Before dismissing this as some quaint historical example of the religious establishment's resistance to change, we must ask: Did it work? The church could well argue that its strategy succeeded, and that Bruno was not burned in vain! Most of the people on the planet still officially behave as though we were the center of the Universe and the only relevant intelligence within it. This remains the anthropocentric doctrine of Judaism, Christianity, and Islam. One can imagine the reluctance of subsequent astronomers to publicize their observations—thereby risking not only Hell, but also an immediate and fiery ticket thereto.

After making examples of Bruno and Galileo, the next layer of information being circulated on observed planetary phenomena probably had a small distribution list, and that within astronomical and astrological circles. Had the respected Galileo's revolutionary findings been fully aired and publicized at the time, the ensuing earthquake might have rocked the very foundations of the Catholic Church. Instead, there have been small and ongoing tremors ever since, with a slow but steady reduction of the Church's power and influence in those areas where it has for longest been established.

Along with the church-fostered geocentric view of the Universe came the doctrine that gOd had not only constructed this beautiful world but he had also done it solely for the human race. He had expressly granted us "dominion over the fish of the sea, and over the fowl of the air, and over the cattle, and over all the earth, and over every creeping thing that creepeth upon the earth," as well as "every herb bearing seed, which is upon the face of all the earth, and every tree," and so on. It says it all, right there in the Bible in the book of Genesis. Ever since, men have been seeking to extend the boundaries of their dominion over this planet and its other inhabitants.

One consequence of this assumption of human dominion over all was to give Christian Western civilization a license to take from this planet with unabashed greed, wiping out species from dodos to whales and destroying entire landscapes and cultures in the process. Humanity was relieved of the need to show any consideration or thought to the land or its other residents, except for their utility to the human race. Other religions such as Hinduism and Buddhism, without this attitude of one gOd doing it all for mankind, often taught respect for other life forms and the land itself, as part of the spiritual path. Those religions certainly have no history of burning or flogging people for communing with our planetary goddess, or for praying to the Sun or moon.

However special and unique is our life on Earth, it seems unlikely that we are the ultimate creation and *raison d'etre* of the infinite Universe that we inhabit, as is implied by the world's major monotheistic faiths. We do seem to be a very special creation of planet Earth, enjoying high intelligence and large brains—attributes which will either save us or destroy us. From the human viewpoint, it has for long appeared as though the evolution of the planet to date had been designed with us in mind. But were the porpoise or eagle to take a similar viewpoint, they might also rationally conclude that this world had been designed with them in mind. Given the opportunity to exchange their free-wheeling lifestyles with that of a human being, they might well choose to stay as they are.

Perhaps we do represent the peak of this planet's evolutionary progress to date. If so, then we have only been at the top of the pile for a few tens of thousands of years, compared to the dinosaur's dominance of over 150 million years. As human beings, naturally biased and unqualified to comment, it is comforting to think that we are the highest life form to exist on Earth. But dolphins and whales are serious contenders, enjoying the benefits of higher intelligence without, as far as we know, suffering from wars, prisons, homelessness, unemployment, or many of the problems that accompany our unique intelligence. What unbridled fun their lives must be, enjoying the gift of life on this planet.

Let us, for the sake of argument, assume that we are the most intelligent species on Earth, and its highest ever manifestation of organic life. Is it not then tragic that, using this intellect, we so blithely and dangerously damage the ecosystem that is our own prime support? Much of the industrialized world's approach to the planet is based upon the simplistic belief that a thoughtful Lord put it all here for us to use—made us the planet's actual owners! The science of astronomy, revealing our insignificance in the grander scheme, makes a mockery of that premise. Yet with unabashed greed our consumer culture continues to pollute the air, the land and the seas with its toxic wastes—all in the course of harvesting the Lord's generous bounty. When we witness our arrogant attitude to the world today, it seems that nearly four centuries later the underlying message of Copernicus, Bruno, and Galileo has still not gotten through.

Religion
is it hard-wired into being human?

THE CURIOUS THING with religion is that, at a fundamental level, it probably does not matter all that much just which of the many creeds a believer chooses to adopt. In a basic way, most religions actually do fulfil a useful purpose, but in the course of it they can also add a lot of misery and mindless mystery to the spiritual process.

So many of today's religions, no matter their god, lay claim to innumerable and sometimes undeniable miracles and signs attesting to their validity. So many practitioners of religion will swear by the positive results they achieve through prayer and supplication to their deities. So many different mantras bring enlightenment and higher states to those who swear by their mantra or method as the only one. How can this be? If only one of these religions has got it right, then everybody else is deluded and wasting their time. Some even believe that the consequence of being "wrong" is condemnation to an eternity of torment—punishment for having listened to the wrong prophets or priests. I don't think so!

Perhaps there exists some kind of a cosmic clearinghouse "up there"—rather like those that handle payments on our various credit and debit cards. At this clearinghouse, it does not matter whether you are Master–JesusCard, BuddhaBank, CityJew, AllahExpress, PaganVista, or a penniless dharma-bum. At this clearinghouse, all devotion to higher beings is accepted, all prayers considered and all meditative and reflective practices rewarded. All gratitude for the wonder of living is received with special relish. The recipient or recipients thereof probably do not care about the detail of what went on in your head to prompt the faith shown by prayer. So what if you've got the divine name completely wrong, or direct your devotions to the flying turtle that is gOd to you—so what if your rituals are not the officially approved ones?

Religion is a candle inside a multicolored lantern. Everyone looks through a particular color, but the candle is always there.
—MOHAMMED NEGUIB

It may not be so important to gOd just when and what you last washed or which bits of hair you choose to grow or cut off. Cleanliness is great (and hygienic), but why should it be close to godliness; where did Jesus shower during forty days of deprivation in the wilderness, while He was getting close to gOd? Which way did Mohammed face to pray before determining that Mecca be the sacred site of Islam? And if your chosen gOd is everywhere and universal, what matters it which direction you face to make your contact? The important factor is, perhaps, that we show gratitude for this creation and the source of our being—seeing both our humility and importance in the cosmic scheme, relishing in and redistributing the love of whatever-you-want-to-call-It.

Our natural and instinctive interest in the meaning of life is one of the decisive factors distinguishing us from other life forms on this planet.[7] Despite this strong inbuilt trait, our consumer culture, analytical intelligence, scientific mindset, and religious dogma have so clouded the issue that we might sometimes be less in touch with the true purpose of our existence than is a common skylark or a towering redwood tree. As the American philosopher Alan Watts would put it, we have ended up in a giant restaurant where we are all sitting around eating the menu rather than the food.

Undoubtedly, some of the religions out there are cleverly constructed confidence tricks, designed to generate fear of a super-being as a means of securing cultural uniformity and submission to authority. Most of to-day's surviving creeds, however, have some basis in original states of ec-stasy and oneness with gOd, together with the revelations, inspirations, and insights that accompany such states. Much of that original spiritual wealth will have survived, undiluted, through centuries of translation, reinterpretation, and tweaking by committees of religious officials. The rest will be colored, tainted, or dated by the time it reached us.

Very often the religious message, though embedded in dogma and doctrine, can be seen to embody essential truths. Many of these truths were becoming recognized long before the advent of organized reli-gions—things like it not being a good idea to kill other people, steal from them, or screw around with their partners. But, using a time-honored technique of propagandists, other more contrived messages are in-cluded with those of innate wisdom or personal resonance. It brings to mind many of the processed foodstuffs that have unnatural additives in-cluded with the basic product, chemicals usually added for the benefit of the producer—not the consumer. Followers of religions are typically told that they must buy into the whole package as instructed, and nei-ther question it, nor play around with other "brands."

With or without religion, you would have good people
doing good things and evil people doing evil things.
But for good people to do evil things, that takes religion.
—STEVEN WEINBERG, 1999

Not many religions offer to put the average believer directly in touch with gOd; to make the connection that is implicit in the Latin root of the word itself. To do this one generally has to join some kind of an "order" (interesting name) and pledge a lifetime of obedience, abandoning the right to free thought and free association in the process.

From time immemorial we have sought means to deal with our basic urge to contact the Other—to be in touch with entities existing in different dimensions to that which we normally experience. Mankind's potential to become involved and even obsessed with things religious can strike all ages, cultures, and sexes. Some will devote their whole lives to religion, while others spend their whole existences tormented by it.

Consider how many more wars have been fought between peoples over differences of religious belief than have been triggered by that other fundamental urge—sex. The only exception that comes to mind is the Trojan War, which was prompted by the abduction of women rather than disagreement over principles or techniques of sex. Though not evident with other mammals, one could almost make the argument that for humanity, religion constitutes a greater instinctive urge than sex. They both appear to be in the same league, though there is no sound reason for them to be in conflict with each other.

This is my simple religion. There is no need for temples; no need for complicated philosophy. Our own brain, our own heart is our temple; the philosophy is kindness.
—DALAI LAMA

Many, understandably, damn all religions on account of the millions who have been slaughtered through the ages in the name of one god or another—sometimes over very small differences of belief. But without their gods, the rulers of the world who have used religion as an excuse to kill and dominate would no doubt have found other justification for their dire deeds. Neither Genghis Khan, Julius Caesar, Joseph Stalin, nor Adolf Hitler relied upon religion as their rationale for killing and conquest. In current times, global conflict is once again being fanned by the winds of religious fundamentalism, though the underlying causes have little to do with spirituality of any flavor.

We should not question the validity of an urge so great as religion—nor can we dismiss all religious thought simply because of the bizarre and irrational ways in which it is often expressed. Perhaps, as with so many other features of our incredibly developed organism, the ability to access gOd is one of our built-in features. If there were a relevance to being in touch with a gOd or other higher beings (many of us certainly think so), then why would this be made such a difficult thing to do? Why should it require learned intermediaries, special clothes, dictated rites and ritual, or years of suffering and contemplation?

Achieving cosmic consciousness and the pure joy and love of being "one with Universe" may not be so easy to do, attainable to all, or relevant to many. But getting in touch with our creator or enabler on a more direct level than priests can do for us should be no more difficult than learning how to whistle, swim, or ride a bicycle. It's about gratitude, acknowledgement, humility, and feedback. That's no new concept. There will forever be variations on where and how the thanks and thoughts are expressed.

Different styles of worship and the issue of who or what we worship and whom we commune with should carry no more weight than different styles of cuisine found in different parts of the world. We can eat well and be healthy on many individual cuisines or on a mix of them, and we can make bad choices and reap ill health and unhappiness from any cuisine. We could be surrounded by the vibrational fields of all manner of consciousness that exists on other scales or dimensions to our own. When saying "Hello" to gods or gOd, surely it is not style that counts, but good thoughts and sincerity.

Much of the practice of religion consists of rites and ritual, performed in the comforting knowledge that previous generations have for long been performing the same rite and ritual. But all traditional practice was once new, when it was first devised as a means to symbolize and express human thoughts and emotions. Sometimes ritual is used to synchronize group activity, bringing together the emotional surges of those present, connecting them all to a greater group experience in the praise of their gods or gOd. The rush experienced by those in such a group is not unlike that felt by fans at peak moments during football games; on the pulsing dance floor of a festival with thousands synchronized to the same beat; or in the orderly ranks of participants at the stirring Nuremberg rallies of Nazi Germany.

Many common rituals apply to most religions. The risk of ordained rituals is that they might be taken as the only means to correspond with whatever god or spirit is being addressed. In some cases worshippers believe they must cross themselves in the correct manner, chant mantras, flick beads, wear special clothes, assume special positions, or face particular directions for their prayers to be received. Surely intent, sincerity, and focus are the first priority, with all else being detail and dressing.

Our lives are full of ritual and many of our daily ones such as eating breakfast, showering, or commuting to work are so familiar to us that we can perform them while carrying on a conversation, planning our day, or listening to the radio news. Unlike our daily ritual routines, those involving spiritual intent should be undertaken with total focus. Otherwise, what is the point?

Religious belief has been used to rationalize all manner of unnatural behavior. We look back in astonishment at the excesses of religious extremism in earlier times yet bizarre practice persists, in some places still enforced by state bureaucracy. During five hundred years of the Inquisition, priests thought it made good sense to torture disbelievers for a few weeks, since it might potentially spare them from an eternity of torment in Hell. It was for their own good. In this century in the United States, people can be imprisoned and have their possessions seized—to protect them from possible damage through puffing a harmless plant they have grown in their own gardens. Countless other absurd victimless "crimes" litter the law books of the world, enforced with fines and imprisonment, this time inflicted by the state instead of the church.

It was once possible for wealthy Catholics to buy "indulgences" from the Church—advance forgiveness for sins they had not yet committed.

Today, if we are famous and rich enough, we buy absolution of those mortal sins in the courtroom. The money goes to expensive lawyers and judges in priest-like outfits instead of to the Church. Once upon a time, voluntarily bequeathing your home to the Church assured you of a place in Heaven when you died. Today, many governments demand a large slice of all the money you ever saved or invested (as in a house), after paying taxes on it during your life. It is called death duty—and a ticket to Heaven is not included.

Many of our ancestors' practices may seem bizarre today, but be assured that from a historic viewpoint many of the practices of today's states and religions will appear equally absurd and insufferable in a hundred years from today. Let us hope, most of all, that our descendants reach the day when they look back with incredulity at the trillion-dollars-plus *of our money* that each year funds the purchase of military technology designed *to destroy us,* our buildings, and our infrastructures. What could be more bizarre than this?

Many of the world's great religious figures made their names through opposing the rite and ritual of the established church of their day. Most of the Jewish prophets, including Jesus of Nazareth, made it their platform and policy to oppose the decadence that periodically took control of the established Jewish religion. Martin Luther founded the Protestant church, seeking to rid Christianity of the rite, ritual, and priesthood of the Vatican. As he embarked upon his quest for enlightenment, the Buddha rejected the strenuous Brahmin ritual and self-mortification that had been inherent to his upbringing. Yet rite, ritual, and organized belief systems seem always to have followed in the wake of the prophets.

To insist on a spiritual practice that served you in the past is to carry the raft on your back after you have crossed the river.

—BUDDHA

The main monotheistic churches maintain a vague concept of just who, what, or where their universal gOd is meant to be. This is surprising when we consider just how many direct conversations their prophets have had with Him. Sometimes we get the image of a big bearded guy who lives in a Heaven that floats in Sun-drenched clouds above Earth. But He is more usually described as an invisible entity by these religions, with little geographical reference to just where He lives.

If the Biblical religions are indeed worshipping the highest imaginable gOd, the one who looks after the known Universe, this is incompatible with a focus upon humanity as the object of His creation. With all the powers He is believed to possess, gOd would not need an entire Universe for the purpose of fostering a species that has existed for just 2 million of the past 13,700 million years. Can we really imagine this Universe-managing entity having a one-to-one conversation with someone down on Earth? Would we ever get one-to-one with one of the beneficial bacteria living in our intestines?

Maybe it is now just too long since the original gOd-connection to tell—too many committees of priests, rabbis, monks, and mullahs down the line from that original enlightenment. The original experience and enlightenment that underlies most churches has been so dogmatized and sanitized that it is difficult to know what really went on in the beginning. It is difficult even to know how much of today's established religions derives from original experience, and how much it absorbed and adapted from the pagan beliefs that were suppressed and supplanted.

The concept of loving the gOd who loves you was often twisted by the church into a "healthy" fear of the Lord—of His judgement and His retribution. In some extreme cases the church, as state, has taken it upon itself to inflict gOd's punishment on the living rather than let them await their retribution in an eternity of Hell. Punishment in parts of Europe, at one time or another, could result from playing music, dancing, worshipping a graven image, missing church, blasphemy, adultery, and much else besides.

It is difficult to say whether organized religions have done more harm than good to humanity in the long term. We can give equal consideration here to the bloodthirsty Aztec Sun priests and the pious Christian priests who urged and took part in their slaughter. Certainly, many millions of individuals have found happiness and increased joy of living through following the maxims and tenets of different religions over the ages. Religion has done much to sustain social organization and standards of morality in many cultures, preserving selective knowledge and providing refuge in troubled times. For this and much else we must sincerely be thankful. But let us bid a simple "Go to Hell!" to all those priests and creeds that preach fear of gOd, with sacrifice and suffering in this life extolled as a means to reach happiness in the next.

In religion and politics people's beliefs and convictions are in almost every case gotten at second-hand, and without examination, from authorities who have not themselves examined the questions at issue but have taken them at second-hand from other non-examiners.

—MARK TWAIN

Organized religion
maybe one of them has got it right

Author's note: Take this chapter as an unbiased alien's overview of organized religions. Should it begin to bore or upset you, then rest assured that you may jump the chapter without in any way hindering your understanding of the rest of the book.

THE YEARS BETWEEN 600 B.C. and 600 A.C. (after Christ) saw the beginning of many of the world's major religions. During this period we saw the flowering of Zoroastrianism and Judaism, together with the births and lives of the Buddha, Confucius, Lao Tzu, Jesus Christ, and Mohammed. Things have never been quite the same since.

All religions contain much that intuitively rings true and noble, combined with much that demands our faith and unquestioning trust. Every master or prophet has been human, with few having anything recorded in their lifetimes. None has had 100 percent clear vision, uninfluenced by personal prejudice and socially accepted norms and forms of the day. Did Abraham, Jesus, or Mohammed have anything much to say about slavery, women's rights, racial prejudice, or pedophiles?[8]

Little of the prophets' original ideas have remained unaltered by multiple translations, cultural traditions and generations of officialdom reinterpreting, rewriting, and building upon previous text. Whether spoken or written, the accumulated words have come to us from the mouths and hands of humans. It is difficult to understand how any book could be expected to contain the authentic and unquestionable "word of gOd"? Yet such is believed by many to be the case.

The majority of today's devout believers will have simply subscribed to the religion of the culture in which they were raised, trusting their parents to have gotten it right. In many cultures there is little choice of spiritual allegiance for those wishing to live in harmony with their family and community. On such a fundamental issue, in many cultures, we find people deliberating more about their automobile or hairstyle than about the religion to which they subscribe. Explore and revel in what is good and beautiful within organized religion, but as Timothy Leary so succinctly put it: "Think for yourself and question authority." Buddha instructed his followers to question even that which they heard from him.

The Hindu religion, predating the prophets' period by anything from two thousand to six thousand years, cannot easily be classed as an organized system of belief, so vast and comfortably contrary are its multiple interpretations. Hinduism enjoys a proliferation of gods and saints, many of whose names are familiar in the West, such as Shiva, Krishna, and Ganesh. It is the world's largest animist religion, believing things to have consciousness that most in the Western world would view as inanimate objects. The Sun god Surya was at one time the highest deity of Hinduism, and is still considered to be so by some schools and swamis.

Hinduism manages to embrace an unlimited selection of flexible and often contradictory rite and ritual. It is difficult to make any broad generalizations about it, and there is nothing in the tradition of Hinduism professing it to be the only route to salvation, or even to a better reincarnation. Unique among major religions, Hinduism has no original founder figure and no creed. Nor has it ever had a central authority determining belief and practice, though Hinduism has long embraced a caste system that seems both odious and iniquitous to those raised in a different culture. It's a funny old world.

Paganism is not organized belief and is not even a religion, though many people credit the term with some form of belief system. In the Middle Ages, it was associated with witchcraft, and pagans risked being burned alive. The term "pagan" originally described a peasant from the country and later came to describe anyone who was not a Jew, Christian, or Muslim. Thus Buddhists, Druids, Incas, Hindus, the ancient Egyptians, Scientologists, and even atheists could all be deemed pagans. The early Gnostics embraced both pagan and Christian elements in their knowledge-based spiritual traditions. It was the open-minded pagan tolerance of spiritual choice that proved to be their downfall at the hands of the intolerant interpreters of the Old Testament.

Once established, the Christians sought out and destroyed pagan cultures of the day, destroying all records of their knowledge, beliefs, and history. After closing pagan universities, the only places of learning that remained were run by Christians.

In common usage today, paganism is usually chosen to describe less structured and non-prophet forms of worship that respect our mother Earth as a goddess, seeing the forces of nature as entities with whom our lives interact. Many of the tenets held by those professing to be pagans today are the same principles underpinning the earliest form of all religion, animism.

Despite the many varieties of religious belief and spiritual practice that preceded Zarathustra Spitama, he is considered to be the first proponent of a supreme gOd—the first organizer. He rose to influence in Persia around the 18th century B.C., though the dating is very inexact. Most followers believe Zarathustra's religion to have been revealed through direct conversations with gOd. His creed is Zoroastrianism, from the Greek translation of Zarathustra.

Today's followers are usually referred to as Parsee, a term derived from the religion's origin in Persia, from where it spread to become the world's first major faith, practiced across an area larger than the Roman Empire. Most of the early history of Zoroastrianism was lost forever when many of its priests, who acted as living libraries, were slaughtered during Alexander the Great's invasion in the 4th century B.C. To the Persians, he was known as "Alexander the Accursed." As a result of this destruction we may never know the identity of the vision-inducing plant Haoma, which was sacred to Zarathustra and his religion. We can be fairly certain, though, that it would be banned today.

The primary creator gOd of Zoroastrians is Ahura Mazda—a god of light and wisdom. He is the source and the fountain of life, the holiest of the heavenly beings who created the Universe. Zarathustra introduced many other new ideas to world religion. Among these were the concept of a force for good fighting against a force for evil; an afterlife for the soul in Heaven or Hell, with a useful in-between zone for borderline cases; and the concept of a final Day of Judgment. The Parsees also recognize lesser gods and regard many aspects of the natural world as possessing spirit, an animistic belief reflected in their worship and ritual, in which both fire and water play integral parts.

Hail to thee, O Haoma, who hast power as thou wilt, and by thine inborn strength! Hail to thee, thou art well-versed in many sayings, and true and holy words. Hail to thee for thou dost ask no wily questions, but questionest direct.

I praise the cloud that waters thee, and the rains which make thee grow on the summits of the mountains; and I praise thy lofty mountains where the Haoma branches spread.

—FROM **YASNA 9 & 10**, ZOROASTRIAN LITURGY
ADDRESSED TO THE SACRED PLANT HAOMA

As well as creating the first universal deity, Zoroastrianism was the first religion that we know to have been ethical, considering goodness (possessing "asha") to be a beneficial factor in life—something to which we should all aspire. A main plank of Zoroastrian belief is that cause and effect are important forces in our lives—we reap what we sow. The primary duties of a Parsee are summed up in the expression: good thought, good words, good deeds.

Zarathustra taught that gOd's divine qualities are manifested in the Universe and our living world. It is a tolerant religion. Upon conquering

Babylon in 570 B.C., Zoroastrian Cyrus the Great created the world's first Bill of Rights, in which slavery was banned, freedom of religion guaranteed and guilt by association with relatives abolished. His victorious soldiers were instructed to respect the private property of those they had vanquished.

The Zoroastrian sphere of influence shrank steadily with the onslaught of militant Islam from the 8th century onwards. From the 10th century onwards, many of the faithful sought refuge in Gujarat, India. A condition of this refuge was their promise not to proselytize, with the consequence that a person can only be born a Parsee, not convert to it. At the time of writing there are only some 250,000 remaining practitioners of this venerable religion.

Curiously, there seems to be no direct lineage or connection between Zarathustra's original supreme gOd and the gOd of the Jews, who was later to become the universal gOd of Christianity and Islam. Nevertheless, those three religions borrowed heavily from the spiritual innovation of Zarathustra.

Lao Tzu was born in China 604 years before Christ and about fifty years before Confucius. He is considered to be the originator of Taoism, which is concerned with following the "Tao," or path. It is centered in right living, determined by inner rules and responsibilities that it is in our interest to understand. Taoists often sought longevity and even immortality through special exercises, potions, and magical objects. Taoism contains little of respect for authority or managed order. Lao Tzu is often considered to be the earliest known anarchist thinker, believing that order and harmony should come from within, as a result of good action, rather than be imposed from without.

Taoism does not concern itself with the nature of god or put forth wise codes of conduct or insist upon ritualized behavior. Taoism is concerned with following the right path through the chaos of existence by making choices that we will not later regret, wherever they lead us. There is not much emphasis on an afterlife, saints, or priests. There have been over thirty translations of Lao Tzu's classic, the Tao Te Ching.

Confucius was not such a laid-back character as Lao Tzu. Politically, he was a conservative, seeking to create social stability by taking soci-

Life is a series of natural and spontaneous changes. Don't resist them—that only creates sorrow. Let reality be reality. Let things flow naturally forward in whatever way they like.

Violence, even well intentioned, always rebounds upon oneself.

When you are content to be simply yourself and don't compare or compete, everybody will respect you.

A leader is best when people barely know he exists, when his work is done, his aim fulfilled, they will say: we did it ourselves.

—LAO TZU

ety back to what had been the status quo. He claimed to have originated none of his own ideas, but to having enshrined in his teachings the virtuous principles that had applied during an earlier golden age. Virtuous conduct was held in high esteem, incorporating the fulfilment of duty to other humans. Hierarchy was very important to Confucius and respect for rulers is fundamental to his teaching. Correct behavior in daily life was considered of great importance and codes for morality, dress, manners, and other matters of social etiquette were strictly laid out. It is not well suited to nonconformists or adventurers, to innovators or hippies.

Though a religion carries his name, Confucius had little interest in spiritual matters or concepts of god. His was a religion confined primarily to matters of ethics and behavior among humans. Confucius gathered a small group of disciples around him, but failed in his attempts to convince either his local rulers or those of other states to adopt his policies. Though he died with his vision unfulfilled, his teachings were outlined in twenty volumes of collected wisdom, called the Analects.

Centuries were to pass before the ruling classes realized their value, and came to support and promote their widespread adoption.

Buddhism has the characteristics of what would be expected in a cosmic religion for the future: it transcends a personal god, avoids dogmas and theology; it covers both the natural and spiritual, and it is based on a religious sense aspiring from the experience of all things, natural and spiritual, as a meaningful unity.

—ALBERT EINSTEIN

Gautama Buddha, who died about 480 B.C., was alive at the same time as Lao Tzu and Confucius. Like Christ, his teachings were verbal and none of his words were committed to writing for at least sixty years after his death (hundreds of years by some accounts). Buddhism seeks to raise us above the illusion that we perceive as our material existence—doing so in a world that quantum physics increasingly perceives as defined by invisible vibration. In doing this, Buddhism does not deny our physical existence nor denigrate it with an assumption of shame and sin. A main goal for Buddhists is to understand life and to achieve detachment from our desire for worldly things. In the pursuit of this ideal, Buddhism has branched into several significantly differing versions with differing approaches to detaching from the material world.

Buddhism is not a theocentric (gOd-focused) religion, and sits comfortably alongside animist worship. There is no concept of heresy or blasphemy. The highest ideal for the Buddhist and the Hindu is to escape "samsara," the karmic cycle of birth and rebirth, and to ultimately live a life of pure spirit. To help them in this, Buddhists venerate a legion of dead saints who reached enlightenment, but stuck around anyway to help the rest of us make the trip.

Buddhism is far simpler than most organized belief systems. There are many Buddhist monks who sustain themselves from alms and charges made to officiate at funerals, weddings, blessings, and other important social occasions. The ideal is to teach Buddhism by example, rather than through preaching and proselytizing. It seems evident, from his own teachings, that the Buddha himself would have been most uncomfortable with the profusion of gold statues venerating his being as well as with Buddhist leaders who become involved in politics, threatening those that are not pious enough. Fortunately, there have been few, if any, wars or massacres committed in the name of the Buddha. The biggest battles Buddhists are meant to wage are with inner emotions and bad attitudes.

Now we come to the three main surviving monotheistic religions: Judaism, Christianity, and Islam. These are all "revealed" religions, in which gOd spoke directly to the prophets and their conversations were infallibly recorded in their holy books. They all believe that their interpretation of gOd is the surest route to salvation, and preach of a struggle between good and evil both in this life and on the spiritual plane. Despite the hostility that has often erupted among and between these belief systems, they all agree on the same universal gOd, share common prophets, and respect the same Old Testament Bible.

Abraham, considered to be a direct descendent of Adam and Eve, is the original prophet to all of them, and their religious officials agree that Jehovah is the same as God who is the same as Allah. They have just been giving different focus to different prophets' interpretations of how He wants us to pay our respects and gratitude; just what lies in store for us after death; what He wants us to do and not do, eat and not eat, grow and not grow, think and not think. The detail of these matters is often invested with great importance. On a broader level, and one enshrined in all three ensuing religions, Abraham specifically spoke out against worship of Sun, moon, or stars.

And of course, there is fear. Possibly as a test of faith, Jehovah commanded Abraham to sacrifice his own son as an offering. Abraham bound his son onto a pyre of wood and was about to plunge in the knife when gOd's messenger told Abraham to stop, because "now I know that you fear God." Abraham is believed to have lived to 175, siring his second son at 99, to a wife aged 90.

The Hebrews spent many years as wandering tribes in the Middle East. Their early religion embraced the animistic attitude of the time, with its followers venerating springs, wells, stone and rock formations, serpents, trees, and demons. Rocks and poles were symbolically placed on hilltops where worship, sacrifice, and gifts of food were made to the spirits of the land—Baals (male) and Asherah (female).

Their religion took new direction after Abraham, with the recognition of a very personal god who looked after the interests of the Hebrews, often in very direct ways. This was tied into the need to observe gOd's specific wishes relating to behavior, diet, and other aspects of life, or risk His displeasure. It was a deal, a binding covenant that both sides were obliged to honor. The Exodus Hebrews knew this god as Yahweh (Jehovah) and he was their god of war, possibly derived from an earlier god of thunder. This religion was significantly bolstered when Moses came down after 40 days without food or water on Mount Sinai, carrying the Ten Commandments and the authority to proclaim the Old Testament as the verbatim word of gOd.

After the successful conquest and occupation of Palestine, Jehovah became installed as the god of this new nation and its people. This god eventually came to be seen as ethical and was thought to be directly involved in Hebrew history—casting out bad kings and replacing them with more obedient ones, turning rivers into blood, parting the Red Sea, sending in locusts, and so on. By 600 B.C. Jehovah's influence had grown considerably, together with that of an elite in charge of religion at the Temple in Jerusalem.

The Jewish prophets sought to redefine the covenant and convey divine messages, often railing at the corruption of the religious establishment, predicting divine retribution, and defining righteous and moral behavior as demanded by gOd. Amos, in the 8th century B.C., became the first prophet to put anything down in writing. He roundly condemned the excesses of the rich and quoted the Lord on how He hated and loathed much of the Hebrew's religious practice. Later on, the prophet Isaiah prophesied that someday people would "not learn war any more" and first proposed the concept of turning "swords into plowshares."[9] We're still waiting.

In the years to come, the narrowly defined god of the Hebrews was redefined by a succession of prophets into a universal "did-it-all" gOd of the Jews. This same gOd, along with some of His prophets, was subsequently adopted by the Christian and Muslim faiths. Judaism does not have any clear ideas on Heaven or Hell, although they do describe an afterlife of everything, nothing, and light. They believe in a Day of Judgment when the Messiah comes to Earth, bringing salvation to all His faithful.

Jews are more concerned with following the Lord's instructions in this life and trusting in Him to reward them how He may. Since this gOd had started out as a specific Hebrew god, the Jews always believed themselves to be his chosen people. Not a lot to ask, considering they had created Him in the first place. Nevertheless, the Jewish religion faced many re-examinations and rearrangements over the centuries as history singled out its followers for an uneven share of human disaster.

By its nature, Judaism is always open to examination and reinterpretation, much of which is expressed as written word and instruction. The definitive work of Judaism, the Talmud, was not completed until about five centuries after the death of Christ.

Christianity began its rise to prominence as a branch of Judaism. Jesus was certainly not the first Jewish prophet to condemn the hypocrisy of the established church of his time and demand change. Nor was he the first to be outraged by how far removed were the priesthood, with their established rites and rituals, from anything holy or connected to a spiritual life. Jesus was crucified for protesting against the Jewish church of the day—the existing religious establishment. The Romans might have tolerated Jesus of Nazareth, but bowed to pressure from the maintainers of the status quo who wanted him out of the picture.

Had Christ survived this episode of his headstrong young prophet phase, he would probably have later become a part of the Jewish tradition, having made a lasting impact on the shape of the faith. But he was sentenced to death instead—martyred to a faith and a church that did not yet exist and would later bear his name. Judaism had experienced and eventually absorbed rebellious prophets before but this one was stopped before even reaching his prime.

The Christianity that we know today did not have an easy birth, and demanded that other interpretations of Christ's teachings be suppressed and eliminated, together with other competing spiritual traditions. Included amongst these were Gnostic groups such as the Ophites, who revered the knowledge-bringing serpent and saw Jehovah as the agent of evil trying to keep us in ignorance of our divine nature. Christian zealots dedicated themselves to destroying every vestige of Gnostic teaching in existence, while instilling their novel concept of built-in sin and the need for salvation. Suffering was to become good for us, and having pleasure was now deemed sinful!

The Church burned enormous amounts of literature. In 391 Christians burned down one of the world's greatest libraries in Alexandria, said to have housed 700,000 rolls. All the books of the Gnostic Basilides, Porphyry's 36 volumes, papyrus rolls of 27 schools of the Mysteries, and 270,000 ancient documents gathered by Ptolemy Philadelphus were burned. Ancient academies of learning were closed. Education for anyone outside of the Church came to an end.
—THE DARK SIDE OF CHRISTIAN HISTORY, **HELEN ELLERBE**

Hundreds of thousands of pagan and Gnostic documents and rolls were burned by these devoutly deranged Christians, as well as the sort of people who wrote or read them. In those days books were not printed, but written or copied by hand, so there were not many to track down and destroy. Most of the knowledge of the ancient world, spiritual and temporal, was lost in the process.

The big leap forward for Christianity came just a few centuries after the death of Christ when the Roman Emperor Constantine, in 313, declared Christianity to be not only permitted, but elevated to most-favored-religion status. He gave powerful political positions to its bishops and the Church became part of the establishment, with its creed being standardized at the Council of Nicea twelve years later. By this time, Christian mobs had begun attacking non-Christian sites, pagan practices were being forbidden, and their temple treasures confiscated by the state and given to the Christian church. There were occasional resurgences of pagan practice but it had now become a life-threatening activity. Even deviations from the authorized Christian belief system were dangerous, as the Cathars were later to discover.

Less than a century after "converting" to Christianity, the great and powerful Rome suffered its first humiliating sacking by barbarians. This traumatic event in 410, at the hands of the Visigoth Alaric, created a state of shock and finger-pointing, with some malignly suggesting that the official imposition of Christianity had something to do with the Empire's decay (even though Alaric himself was a Christian). St. Augustine, then a famous Bishop in North Africa, was charged with defending the religion. In successfully doing so, he remodelled the church along the centrally controlled lines of the Roman Empire. No longer were individuals to be trusted with their own spiritual well-being or allowed to have a direct and personal understanding of the teachings of Jesus. These matters were now considered beyond the intellectual capacity of the average man, and best left to the priesthood for interpretation and guidance.

Instead of the Emperor, the church now had the Pope as its infallible leader. Rome was to be rebuilt from its ruins along Christian lines, with fear and punishment employed as the church's official weapons in its battle against the inherently sinful nature of man. It was a clever scam, declaring war on an undefined evil that is lurking within us and then consuming our freedom in the ensuing battle—all done in order to save us from the terrors of Hell. Sound familiar?

Eventually, in the name of the Savior Jesus, countless disbelievers were to be cruelly slaughtered by the righteous as they sought to spread His word throughout the known world and into new ones. When the victorious army of the holy First Crusade sacked Jerusalem in 1099, they massacred about 70,000 men, women, and children who believed that

Mohammed was the better interpreter of the same gOd's wishes.[10] The local Jews, coexisting with the dominant Muslims, were singled out to be burned alive.

Little more than a century later, the Albigensian Crusade set out to eliminate every vestige of the Cathar religion, a simple form of Christ's teachings tracing its lineage to Mary Magdalene. As the Crusaders entered the besieged city of Beziers, in what is now the south of France, their Papal leader was asked how to distinguish the Catholics from the Cathars in the city of 30,000. His historic answer sealed the fate of every man, woman, and child within the walls: "Kill them all—God will recognize his own." The Inquisition was subsequently conceived in order to seek out and neutralize Cathars elsewhere who had seen what happened in Beziers and fled. When they ran out of Cathars, they found others to persecute.

A few centuries later, more adventurous Christians would wreak havoc and horror upon the native inhabitants of the new worlds they "discovered." Heavily armed gold-loving Christians claimed these territories in the name of their kings or queens, finding reasons to slaughter those who opposed their wholesale theft of gold, silver, and valuables. But they brought these newly impoverished populations the possibility of salvation, by teaching them and their children Christianity.

There are many in today's world who can bear testament to the havoc, horror, and impoverishment delivered by devout and highly armed Christians. This time around they are oil-loving Christians, bearing the gift of social salvation to be achieved through the enlightened imposition of democracy.

How long can this scam continue?

I have recently been examining all the known superstitions of the world, and do not find in our particular superstition (Christianity) one redeeming feature. They are all alike founded on fables and mythology.

—THOMAS JEFFERSON

Perhaps Christians should be grateful to the Jews for their involvement in the death of Jesus. Without the crucifixion they would lose one
of the core tenets of Christianity: that by ending up nailed to a cross,
Jesus absolved us of sin. We must question where is the sense in this
peculiar notion? GOd sends His only son to Earth in order to teach us
about the love, the truth, and the intentions of his father. This stretches
the imagination, but let's go with it for a minute. His son grows up as
an unknown carpenter until his early thirties, when his mission in life
is manifested and he sets forth spreading the word of the Lord. After
less than three years on this path, he upsets the religious establishment
and is sentenced to death by the colonizing Romans. As was the cus-
tom, he is nailed to a cross and left overnight to die of exhaustion and
suffocation.

This is a terrible thing for us to have done—nail up gOd's only loving son just as he is reaching the prime of his life. How can logic be so
twisted as to propose that, in response to this ungrateful deed, gOd absolved us of all sins past (whatever religion we had been), and from sins
of the future (providing we were good Christians)? Surely if gOd wants
to absolve us of our sins on Earth he could just do it, without needing
to have His only son cruelly sacrificed by us as a result of spreading His
word. There's some very twisted thinking going on here, but hey, dying
young has never gotten in the way of achieving everlasting fame.

In any event, many are convinced by evidence suggesting Jesus survived the ordeal of crucifixion and ended his days in Kashmir, preaching
away to the age of 120. And there are those who assert that most of the
Jesus story is an artificial construct, noting striking similarities between
events in Jesus' life and those of various Sun-related god and demi-god
characters who preceded him, from the Egyptian Horus to the Persian
Mithra. Many superhero celebrities of antiquity were described as being
the children of Zeus or other randy gods; "son of god" was not a unique
concept.

Disenchantment with the religious establishment became widespread
by the 16th century, with a corrupt church elite promising forgiveness
and guaranteed access to Heaven for those with money enough to pay
for it. Martin Luther was so appalled by corrupt Papal practices that

he initiated one of the worlds first major protest movements: the Protestant Church, a momentous break from the established order of the Roman Catholic Church and the power of the priesthood. Since then, many battles and wars have been fought between Christian and Christian over differences of belief and interpretation. Many have followed in Luther's footsteps, becoming disenchanted with the established religious options and developing new versions—from the Church of the Latter Day Saints to the Branch Davidians who were burned to death in Waco, Texas.

When I was a kid, I used to pray every night for a new bike. Then I realized that the Lord doesn't work that way, so I stole one and asked Him to forgive me.
—PETER KAY, BRITISH COMEDIAN

The world today boasts countless variants on Christianity, tens of thousands according to some estimates, with the newest ones always being thought of as the most strange and wacky. However, after fifteen hundred years or more of Christian spiritual domination over much of Europe, more people have simply given up on it altogether. It seems to them increasingly unlikely that any new variation of this old and heavily organized belief system is going to bring about the goals that Jesus Christ had in mind. There is, of course, a downside to this as any good spiritual advice and sound social principles that Jesus conveyed to us risk being thrown away along with centuries of artificial additives and grossly modified ideas.

Far younger than Christianity, Islam has not reached the phase of widespread disillusionment or disinterest that accompanies most aging religions. Mohammed entered the scene 570 years after Christ and managed to develop Islam into a major religion within his own lifetime—an achievement that most prophets would just die for. He began his life as an orphan and then went into business managing camel caravans before marrying a wealthy widow.

Mohammed was a man of excellent reputation, and became a prophet at the age of forty after a curious exchange with the archangel Gabriel. In this visitation the angel kept urging him to "read", while the illiterate Mohammed responded, "I cannot read." He was shaken by this first experience, thinking for a while that he might be going mad. But after a few repeat episodes, and solid support from his wife, Khadija, he came to believe that Gabriel was conveying the unquestionable words of gOd to him. Mohammed placed himself in the line of prophets progressing from Noah to Abraham, Moses, and Jesus, claiming to be the final messenger of the same gOd—the last prophet and the only one with the perfectly correct message.

The punishment for those who wage war against Allah and His Prophet and make mischief in the land, is to murder them, crucify them, or cut off a hand and foot on opposite sides...their doom is dreadful. They will not escape the fire, suffering constantly.

—KORAN 5.33

Though illiterate himself, much of the ongoing message spoken through Mohammed was written down while he lived, a rare luxury for any prophet. The Koran itself was assembled from these messages within a few decades of his death, to form the core bedrock of the Islamic faith. The other major, though secondary, book of Islam is the Hadith, which contains a record of what Mohammed is believed to have said and done in his life. This was painstakingly assembled over a long period, beginning a century after the death of the prophet. Both of these books contain a considerable amount of advice and instructions on worship, daily living, what to eat, what to wear, and how to behave in society.

One is not supposed to breathe or blow into a drinking vessel, nor ever leave a fire lit in the house when going to sleep. Eating any part of a pig is forbidden unless your life depends upon it, and even an aspiring holy martyr must settle his debt at the local kebab shop before sacrificing his life. Debtors are not allowed in Heaven.

True believers in Islam are certain that their holy books contain the words and reflect the instructions of an omnipotent gOd who deals punishment when his will is not obeyed and rewards when it is. Strict adherence to the instructions of the Koran and Hadith is considered to be the surest route to Heaven. The Heaven described by Islam is sometimes considered to be male-oriented, with an afterlife attended by beautiful houris (nymphs of paradise) and the ability to drink forbidden wine without suffering any ill effects. All this is enjoyed in a body restored to the peak of youthful fitness. Holy martyrs get special treatment in this Heaven, though one must wonder whether the martyred children of Palestine will appreciate all those willing virgins and the unlimited wine.

Mohammed introduced the concept of jihad (holy war) and became its first conquering warrior, victoriously leading his armies into battle. With Allah firmly by their side, Muslim armies sacked and pillaged much of what they conquered, slaughtering infidels up to 100,000 at a time, while pressing widows and orphans into slavery. Hindus suffered terribly at their hands under occupation, reeling in disbelief at the Muslims' capacity to inflict horror upon other humans. Islam at one time or another subjugated all of North Africa, the Middle East, most of India, and large chunks of Europe and China. Most of Islam's newly conquered subjects were given the choice of conversion to Islam or death. Since Jews and Christians worshipped the same gOd, they often received the softer option of either converting, or paying penalty taxes and suffering social discrimination.

Despite the assiduous following of their gOd's prophet-delivered instructions over the centuries, there has been no shortage of bloody and brutal conflict between Muslim and Muslim, even between those of the same sect. In this practice, they are not unlike Christians.

In its early centuries, Islam stressed the value of an open and enquiring mind, maintaining and developing what remained of the scientific knowledge of earlier cultures—salvaging that which had survived Christian destruction. Scholars were held in high esteem and great cities prided themselves on attracting the best astronomers and mathematicians to their fold. Ironically, the scientific knowledge that Islam maintained and developed provided the foundations for the cultural and technological revolution that eventually lifted a Christian Europe out of its dark ages and into the Renaissance.

It is not fitting for a Muslim man or woman to have any choice in their affairs when a matter has been decided for them by Allah and His Messenger. They have no option. If any one disobeys Allah and His Messenger, he is indeed on a wrong Path.
—**KORAN 33.36**

Like most religions, and more so than most today, Islam does embody a clear code of conduct for society, which, in an Islamic state, can be established as the law and regulation of the country. Sharia, the unquestionable divine law, can demand that a transgressor be flogged for flirting, stoned to death for adultery, or spend years behind bars for selling alcohol. Divine guidance is even dispensed on the appropriate number of lashes to be given in punishment for specific misbehavior. If this seems harsh or shocking, we must remember that Islam is 600 years younger than Christianity.

A few hundred years ago, pious Christians burned witches and heretics at the stake in Europe. Spain's Catholic Inquisition was likely to torture and possibly torch those accused of being "closet" Jews or Muslims—just posing as Christians to secure social advantage. Such was the fear of this happening that ham and all forms of pig meat, forbidden to Jews, became the national diet in much of Spain, and remains so to this day.

Five hundred years ago in civilized Geneva, attendance at Calvin's Protestant church was enforced by law. Adultery, blasphemy, and heresy were punishable by death, and for 100 years no music or musical instrument was allowed in the city. Let us hope that humanity will not have to wait 600 years for Islam to mellow. And yes, this sort of behavior is, as it was, harsh and shocking.

The real problem, then, is not with the basic fundamentals of worship, gratitude, and guidelines for social conduct. The real problems arise when they become mandated by intolerant zealots as compulsory, unquestionable practice. "You will live your life on Earth as directed by gOd or face the consequences on Earth—never mind your after-life." Can we believe that a gOd who is responsible for the known Universe would get involved in the detail of what we do with our body hair, who we have sex with, or how many times we should be whipped for whatever?

Problems arise when religions become rigidly organized and open to central control—for the spiritual benefit of the people, of course. The control of religion can be achieved geographically, as it did when existing pagan sites were renamed by the church after Christian saints. Spiritual pilgrims had venerated Mecca as a sacred site for pagan practices long before Mohammed occupied it by force on behalf of Islam.

More commonly the priesthood will intellectually manage access to religion. They achieve this by codifying, complicating, and obfuscating the fluid dynamics of our relationship with an intelligent Universe. The result is that we end up believing that their priests, monks, mullahs, and rabbis—their creeds, codices, and rituals—are necessary intermediaries between us and the lofty notions of gOd that only they can decipher. The more rules, rites, and regulations they get down on paper, the more credibility they seem to acquire.

I have spent much of my life learning of the connection between what we eat and what we are, and one thing is certain: there is no such thing as a perfect diet that will suit everyone, or even the same person all the time. We are all different and, though we do better to eat some foods than others, we are free to make the choices ourselves and enjoy or suffer the consequences. It is the same with religion—there is good substance in most religions, but there is no one detailed spiritual path that fits all.

> *I do not believe in the creed professed by the Jewish church, by the Roman church, by the Greek church, by the Turkish church, by the Protestant church, nor by any church that I know of. My own mind is my own church.*
> **—THOMAS PAINE,** *AGE OF REASON,* 1794

We have good cause to appreciate the many sound moral principles and social ethics that are contained within and promoted by religions. It is a great shame that they have suffered so many scoundrels in their midst and brought themselves into such disrepute. In the final analysis, however, we must come to recognize that loving our neighbors, being charitable and respecting life, for example, are sound principles that benefit us all. When we are commanded to love our neighbor because gOd or his agents have instructed us to do so, then we are in danger of not appreciating the intrinsic value of the act itself.

At least all religions (almost) agree on one thing—the Golden Rule.

Zoroastrianism
That nature alone is good which refrains from doing unto another whatsoever is not good for itself.
DADISTAN-I-DINIK, 94,5

Brahmanism
This is the sum of duty: Do naught unto others which would cause you pain if done to you.
MAHABARATA, 51 1517

Buddhism

Hurt not others in ways that you yourself would find hurtful.

UDAN-VARGA, 5,18

Judaism

What is hateful to you, do not to your fellow men.
That is the entire Law; all the rest is commentary.

TALMUD, SHABBET, 31A

Christianity

All things whatsoever ye would that men should do to you,
do ye even so to them: for this is the Law and the Prophets.

MATTHEW 7:12

(The emphasis on doing, rather than not doing is highly significant.)

Islam

No one of you is a believer until he desires for his brother
that which he desires for himself.

SUNNAH

("Brother" is generally used to address fellow Muslims.)

Confucianism

Surely it is the maxim of loving-kindness: Do not unto
others that you would not have them do unto you.

ANALECTS, 15.23

Taoism

Regard your neighbor's gain as your own gain,
and your neighbor's loss as your own loss.

T'AI SHANG KAN YING PIEN

Jainism

In happiness and suffering, in joy and grief,
regard all creatures as you would regard your own self.

YOGA-SASTRA

Animism: first faith
perhaps our instincts make more sense

THERE WAS a time when we did not have such knowledge of the world around us, and how it works the way it does. We did not understand the chemical process of combustion or the makeup of a flame. Fire was a great mystery to us, even after we learned to manage and maintain it. We knew nothing of the delicate cellular requirements for organic life—or of the neurological structures of our brain, which enable us to experience our existence. We assumed that fire had a life of its own, and that all manner of other things were able to experience their own existence, whether or not they had brains, eyes, and blood-filled veins.

Our Stone Age ancestors had not yet intellectually separated themselves from the ecosystem called Earth—had not elevated themselves to a status above and separate from all else upon this planet—assuming a status greater than the planet itself or the Sun above. Perhaps they remembered deep inside of the time not so distant when they were more likely to be the hunted than the hunter; when they were prey for larger carnivores and omnivores. They would have been more conscious than are we of the nonexclusive nature of consciousness itself.

It seemed apparent, then, that all things shared in the pervasive life force that we ourselves enjoy. Spirit was seen to be everywhere, in the ground beneath our feet and in all the living things upon it—even in the rivers and oceans, the hills and the mountains. It seemed reasonable to assume that something as organized, purposeful, and individual as a river might also share the sensations of being and self-awareness that we experience.

Without today's tools and technologies engaging and distracting us, we were more aware and in touch with all around us. We had to be, for without today's tools and technologies protecting and managing us, we could not so well insulate ourselves from the influence of chance and fortune. There existed a common acceptance that the behavior we displayed in our lives in some way influenced the behavior of the natural world surrounding us. Though nobody saw it as religion then, independent belief systems developed around the world, often sharing common traits. Similar ceremonies were performed to encourage the rain, promote successful childbirth, or to correct poorly performing fruit trees—in all parts of the world.

I borrowed a common ritual from Sir James Frazier's seminal compilation of ancient ritual, *The Golden Bough*. It was designed to prompt a nonperforming apple tree of mine to bear good fruit for the first time in six years, using a ceremony documented in Malaysia, Japan, and Bulgaria. The ceremony involves having one person in the tree with an axe, threatening to cut the "useless" thing down and another on the ground pleading for its life, begging just one more year from the would-be executioner. It prompted fruit-bearing for another two years.

The sort of activities Sir James catalogues that involve communication with non-human entities and forces are now commonly dismissed as superstition. Superstition is defined by *Collins Dictionary* as "irrational belief usually founded on ignorance." The belief by mariners that the phases of the moon were related to tidal flows was long dismissed as superstition by the scientific establishment, until Sir Isaac Newton discovered of the laws of gravity.

We were once completely enveloped by the natural world and more intimately in touch with it than we are today. In this modern high-tech culture we give little thought to the natural world, cocooned as we are in our moving vehicles, centrally heated buildings, and concrete cities. Instead, we entrust science and technology to understand, tame, and harness the world's weirdness and wildness. We heat our environment in the winter and cool it in hot summer; we have water on tap and buy food at the shop; the power of ancient Sunlight comes out of wires in the wall; we fly in comfort and safety over rugged mountain ranges and raging oceans. We exclude as much as possible the elements of risk, chance, and uncertainty from our lives. We have a tendency to see ourselves as different, apart and superior to all other physical inhabitants of the world—as being in control. Yet when a tsunami approaches, it is all the other animals who run for the high ground.

Science has to a degree replaced religion, which once held a monopoly on explaining all the mysteries of the world. But science does not study the greatest mystery of all—spirit—choosing instead to vigorously deny its existence. Most scientists believe our perception of life force and consciousness to be no more than crafty illusions of the brain, presumably developed to somehow provide genetic advantage. If we want advice or information about this area we most commonly turn to priests, monks or spiritual teachers of some kind. There is a wealth, and variety, of material available today seeking to explain the nature of spirit and the afterlife. It was not always so.

What was going on before we were given all the explanations? Our ability to passionately believe in the unsubstantiated did not suddenly appear from nowhere. What was going on during this time to satisfy the spiritual urges of our species—a time when, presumably, there was nobody but gOd in the Christian Heaven? Organized religions did not just spring into being in the wake of the prophets. Instead, they built upon and often supplanted belief systems and moral codes that had been in existence long before them. People had already figured out many of the basic lessons contained within organized religion. Like the porpoise, wildebeest, or crow, we are a community animal and therefore naturally designed to figure out how to live together and co-exist in groups, without the absolute need for tablets from gOd, prophets or the services of a global policeman.

We have had religion in our lives since long before the prophets came onto the scene speaking thus and that and lo'ing and beholding. From a time long ago, when we acquired spare time to reflect, it seems that an interest in the mysteries of life, death, and the world of spirit has been a hallmark of our species. We have always been interested in that "Other" world of invisible forces and influences, and in finding means to harness it and work in harmony with it. Just as Stone Age peoples had no name for their own period in history, so the precursors to organized religion had no all-embracing name for their mode of belief. Today we call it animism. Everything in this world was then perceived to have spirit or consciousness in varying degree, regardless of whether growing and moving about, like we do, formed a part of its existence. That is to say, rocks, hills, rivers, mountains, winds, currents, oceans, as well as animals and plants of all sorts were seen as having an awareness of their own existence in this world. Everything was seen to partake in the life-force energy present in a living world.

Honor the sacred.
Honor the Earth, our Mother.
Honor all with whom we share the Earth:
Four legged, two legged, winged ones,
swimmers, crawlers, plant and rock people.
Walk in balance and beauty.
—NATIVE AMERICAN ELDER

This universal energy has been called Chi and Holy Spirit and other names in other cultures—that old invisible divine life force of which we perceive ourselves to be a manifest part. There was an intuitive perception that various invisible energies and entities were somehow in an active interface with the visible physical world that we inhabit. It was commonly thought possible to influence events around us by methods other than mechanical interventions on the physical level. And this belief and practice did not exist because it was written about, taught in schools or legislated by government. It arose from innate instincts and

basic understanding, in stark contrast to many of today's entrenched belief systems.

In many cultures it was, and occasionally still is, the role of the shaman to travel into the spirit world, exploring varied dimensions of existence and communicating with plants, animals, and other entities.
Though rare individuals have the ability to easily cross between the material and spirit worlds, the majority of shamans employ techniques to
make the journey. These can involve hours of strong dancing, weeks of
fasting, years of meditation, ingestion of potent psychedelic plants, ritual drumming, self-mortification, and more. There are those who seek to
dismiss these altered states as false and fabricated experiences, triggered
simply by changes to the body's chemistry. Yet to dismiss them as arti-
ficially induced is to ignore that similar experiences arise from a multitude of techniques, and across disparate cultures.

One way or another, wherever people gathered on the planet, a means
was usually found to tap into an Other world for religious experience
and spiritual guidance. The shaman will learn from the tradition of the
craft, using time-honored techniques to create a personal interface with
the world of spirit, seeking knowledge and guidance directly from the
Source. This is in contrast to the approach taken by priest-types who rely
primarily upon the spiritual experiences of others, as filtered, translated,
and re-interpreted throughout centuries or millennia of transmission.

Many forms of animist practice still abound around the world: em-
bodied as an integral part of India's Hinduism, or Shinto in Japan; alongside a tolerant Buddhism; as traditional native practice; or curiously
incorporated into Christianity's highly adapted congregations of Africa
and South America. Many notable sites, long considered to hold spiritual powers, were commandeered and Christianized with the spread of
the church—becoming reborn or rechristened as the spring or rock of St.
Whoever. But some special spirit existed in this location and was recognized long before Jesus or any of his followers walked upon Earth, or
water.

Animism, strange though it may appear through the eyes of modern
culture, must have seemed literally second nature to us in those times.
Invisible entities were thought to play an integral part in our destiny.

They might intervene in perverse or poetic ways—at times guiding and rewarding us, and at others mocking our foolishness or sabotaging best-laid plans.

Communicating to invisible entities that inhabited either physical or spiritual space was common stuff. There were many spirits to choose from, some of them representing places, whether a local holy spring, a mountain, or the moon. Others would embody the force of lightning, the caretaker of agriculture, or a sacred animal. Spirits arose representing powerful phenomena such as love or war. Some of these spirits were seen as gods, such as Venus and Mars. Worshipping spirit entities and communicating with them still is, of course, the basic stuff of most churches. It is just expressed in a more organized and regulated manner towards demons, angels, and the spirits of countless saints, not forgetting the long-dead Jesus and his mom and Dad.

Trees, especially the oak, were accorded great respect throughout Europe, which had once been almost entirely covered by these lords of the vegetable kingdom. To quote Sir James Frazier in *The Golden Bough*:

How serious that worship was in ancient times may be gathered from the ferocious penalty appointed by the old German laws for such as dared to peel the bark of a standing tree. The culprit's navel was to be cut out and nailed to the part of the tree which he had peeled, and he was to be driven round and round the tree till all his guts were wound about its trunk. The intention of the punishment clearly was to replace the dead bark by a living substitute taken from the culprit; it was a life for a life, the life of a man for the life of a tree.

Sir James neglects to tell us whether this curious practice was ever credited with restoring the tree to health.

Though regarded as high entities, trees were not considered to be gods. As with many things of a spiritual nature, there is a fuzzy line defining the boundary at which a spirit reaches or deserves god status. A prime determination would be how much power or life force the candidate is perceived to have. Having a good critical mass of believers must also be a useful factor. God status was commonly given to Sun; the moon; other planets of this solar system; to major phenomena of the world such as oceans, agriculture, and weather; to human emotions and creations such as love, family, and war. Those living near an active volcano might come to believe that it had vastly more spirit than puny and transient human beings, and seek means to contact and influence it.

In a world over which we had far less control, we sought means to supplicate those visible and invisible factors that were thought to have an influence upon our lives. We wanted assistance, or at least coopera-tion, from entities not even recognized today.[11] Many of the early spir-its, demons and local gods were seen as inhabitants of and connections to another type of world—a world that was able somehow to influence events in this one. And they provided useful receptacles for gratitude, supplication, devotion, or unknowing fear. There were shamans then, to help us tune into the Other, but there were no psychotherapists, and per-haps less need for them when humanity was still living in cognizance of a world that exists in a place beyond television, physical existence, and material wealth.

Without a need for central control, animism provides for multiple forms of worship and contact with different phenomena, both physi-cal and non-physical. Some holy places or spirits would have received more attention than others—cults would develop and grow larger and become organized. The first proto-priests may have arisen through act-ing as the official custodians of holy places and as the purveyors of rec-ommended ritual.

There is little more than cave art, archeological artefacts and informed conjecture to inform us of human culture in the period up to around 3000 B.C. About that time cities and states began to develop with a bu-reaucracy maintaining "written" records (usually for tax purposes). The priesthood was now high in the power structure, acting as conduit to the gods, and developing more complex and formalized rite and ritual. I would wager that the priesthood is the oldest profession on this planet and that it long preceded prostitution, eventually even contributing to society's need for the latter through the constraint of our primitive and instinctive sexuality.

Animism recognized an endless variety of spirit entities in countless cultures, eventually providing employment for a multitude of shamans, and priest-types responsible for ceremony and special sites. Despite the variety of belief, in most of the world's earliest religions it was common to revere Sun as a major and often primary god. Earth goddess Sophia once figured large in the pantheon of early gods but fared badly at Christian hands, being effectively replaced by a subservient Virgin Mary. The oldest surviving animist religions on the planet are Hinduism and Zoroastrianism, both having origins earlier than 1500 B.C. Both venerate gods representing phenomena, especially those of Sun and of the light transmitted through it. The religion of ancient Egypt fully embraced animism in its worship of many gods, including Sun.

Yet it was Egypt that hosted the world's first known appearance of monotheism, during the reign of Amenhotep IV, during the 14th century B.C. This pharaoh, husband to Nefertiti, believed Sun-god Aten to be a one and only gOd, and changed his name to Akhenaten out of respect (meaning "servant of Aten"). He banned worship or display of all other Egyptian gods, ordering the destruction of their temples and images. This represented a huge cultural change to ancient Egypt, casting out polytheism for the first time in history, and several theories seek to explain the basis of this shift. Akhenaten dramatically changed the style of Egyptian art, and even built an entirely new capital city. The Egyptian priesthood, who had previously been employed to represent a wide array of gods, were understandably upset by these changes and, after Akhenaten's death, soon reestablished the old animistic beliefs on which they traded. Some subscribe to the theory that Akhenaten paved the way, and even provided inspiration, for the one and only gOd of Moses.

Sun was usually to be found within the pantheon of any society's gods regardless of culture and geography—as long as they had not come under the influence of Judaic, Christian, or Muslim religions. Sun had countless personas: to the Yokut Indians, it was created by the coyote from a magic fire; according to the Inuit, it was a young brother to the female moon; it was often the husband or brother of the moon, and in a few cultures the genders were reversed with the moon being male and Sun female. For many, it was seen as the most important god.

Solar worship of any sort is clearly animist. Sun, for all its complex and beneficial activity, is now widely perceived as an inanimate and accidental event in space from which we just happen to benefit. Thus, to invest it with spirit falls within the animist camp.

From a century before Christ until 313, the major religion of the Roman Empire was animist, worshipping the Sun god Mithra, adapted from the Zoroastrian tradition. Very little is known of this highly secretive religion, which had many members in the Roman army; included slaves who might rise higher in the church than their master; and which excluded women. Mithra's birthday was December 25 and Sundays were dedicated to him. When Christianity supplanted it as the official Roman religion in the 4th century A.D., Mithraism came in for official suppression by the new status quo, and disappeared by the end of the 5th century.

Whether we worship the son of an invisible gOd, the tangible Sun, Beelzebub, flying turtles, or our local volcano, when worship becomes organized, mystified, and managed by priest-types with rites and ritual, things can get strange and twisted, regardless of the god, prophet, or initial concept. Perhaps worship itself brings a kind of blindness with it, in contrast to the clearer vision that comes through respect, gratitude, and recognition. Worship creates an illusion of separation, whereas everything at play with us in this earthly sphere is acting and reacting with everything else on a continual basis—independently and unpredictably. The plot is generated as we progress, and we all of us have a hand in it. It is a flowing system that can only stagnate in the face of efforts by a hierarchy to organize it deterministically.

With human beings, the nature of each receipt and response with the spirit world must be channelled through the subtle electromagnetic energies of our brains. This brain activity itself is probably only a conduit for the even subtler energies at play in our mind. It is easy to overlook the fact that the essence of us, our own spirit and consciousness, is also a part of the invisible world—that part which makes our complicated body alive. It is no wonder our species has for thousands of years found it easy to believe in the invisible, however the belief may be derived or channelled, and however difficult it is to substantiate scientifically.

We like to think that the chaos is under our control—that we have screened out the possibility of any "outside" interference with our best-laid plans. To a large degree this is true, as we rely more and more on the efficiency of machines to manage our lives. But perhaps inanimate phenomena and invisible entities are still able to interact with our reality, albeit at a very subtle level. The slightest electromagnetic signal might provide enough stimuli to direct a glance, or prompt a pause, raise a memory, make a connection, or fumble and drop. A common example seems to occur soon after that point when we finally give up on looking for something, or have obtained a replacement for it, at which time it suddenly "reveals" itself to us. How many times has an unexpected encounter, a chance glance, or an out-of-the-blue phone call occurred at the precise moment needed to discover something, complete a mission, or save the day?

During their lifetimes every man and woman will stumble across a great opportunity. Sadly, most of them will simply pick themselves up, dust themselves down, and carry on as if nothing ever happened.
—**SIR WINSTON CHURCHILL**

It is foolish to dismiss as chance those million-to-one synchronicities that we so frequently encounter. We could add an entire appendix full of these to this book but I am sure you will be familiar with the phenomenon. They are the source of countless "You won't believe what happened" stories—often adding poetry, irony, perfect timing, humor, or any mix thereof to the ongoing present as it matures from the chance and choices of our past presence. The prevailing scientific mindset would have us believe that these events are all driven by chance alone. But might they be influenced by phenomena and objects we view as inanimate and a spirit we consider to be implausible?

Many of the great discoveries of science have been triggered by the recognition and further investigation of a timely "chance" accident—by synchronicity. It is likely that there would be even more such "accidental" discoveries were more scientists open to such inexplicable assistance and looking for them as they work.

The tiniest tweaks of fate (some may call it chance) have so often undermined the best-laid plans or brought together everything required when nothing but intent was there. We do well to recognize these influences in our lives and realize thereby the reality of our connection to an unseen world of spirit. If warnings are given, then listen to them. If thanks are warranted, then give them. No particular ritual is required or more important than our simple grateful awareness—something for which no formal training is required.

We should also acknowledge, in hindsight, those times that inexplicable phenomena tried to stop us from doing something and we proceeded against these strange obstacles, to our subsequent regret. Mundane as it is, when I have trouble getting a letter to print, like the paper jamming or a loose connection, I'll take another look at it and usually find out that I've done something like saying "Dear Harry" in a letter that has been written to Hilary. Listen more closely next time and learn to differentiate between the challenging obstacle begging to be overcome, and the signal to examine what's being done.

We receive, or at least are offered, far more direction in following our path through this life than is immediately apparent. Of course, there will always be times when we are deflected from our path and undermined in its pursuit, and at these times we should look within and question why.

Guardian angels, bad-luck demons, and all sorts of entities, from the highest divinity to a humble geographical site, have been perceived as capable of affecting our existence for as long as we have records of human culture. The nature of these influences was clearer to animist pre-prophet society than it is to our own, brought up as we are to view the world as our personal unthinking supply cupboard. The world's major organized religions still maintain the concept of influence from inanimate objects and a world of invisible beings. It's just that most of them insist that the only invisible entities in existence are their own designated ones, and that these only respond to accredited practices.

Invisible entities and the invisible energies of inanimate objects can play a subtle and sometimes significant part in our lives regardless of our adherence to any particular belief system, whether spiritual or scientific. But too often their silent signals go unnoticed, drowned out by the incessant diversions of our information and entertainment-driven culture.

It does seem like our species once had the natural skills needed to associate with other beings in both subtle and straightforward ways. Our ancestors throughout the world once spent time connecting with inanimate phenomena and invisible entities, believing that they were getting value from the exchange. Today we are taught to look on this activity as wasted time, prompted by delusional beliefs. At the same time, we happily live on lifeless processed food, manage our mental state with pharmaceuticals, and satisfy our community instincts by watching imaginary people's lives unfold on screen. And we bemoan our lack of control over both global events and our own lives.

Perhaps the animistic communication skills we once enjoyed have been erased from our genetic makeup through generations of disuse, misuse, and abuse. Or perhaps we are just very, very out of practice.

Sun of gOd:
our local life transmitter

I N THIS SMALL patch of galaxy there would be naught but
empty space without Sun acting as our local broadcaster—
beaming the power of the light throughout its solar system
and beyond. It fills this space with energy and is, perhaps, the primal bat-
tery behind all other forms of energy from bolts of lightning to thought
itself. It is solar gravity that holds the family of planets together and it is
solar energy that builds and powers the incredible variety of living organisms on this planet. Still, many pass through their day without giving a second thought to Sun—to that which played the greatest part in
making the day possible, and all the days before.

Without the electromagnetic entity that is our Sun there would be
nothing here, there would be no solar system, no us, nor even place for
a humble grain of sand. There would be nothing at all but nothingness,
occasional patches of thin gas and the twinkle of distant stars. Perhaps
a universal spirit, if such exists, would pervade even the nothingness of
outer space, but surely it would manifest at higher orders when channelled through a blazing star.

Many years before starting on this book, it occurred to me that Sun,
our own personal star, might be an entity of sorts. For years I entertained
the idea as an intellectual possibility, there being no particular "Eureka!"
point. But eventually an initial inkling grew into a conviction that we are
daily in the presence of a celestial being, in the literal sense of the word.

It now makes sense that Sunshine seems so palpably full of life and up-lifting vibrations, and that however fierce and scorching it might get at noon in the desert, it is rarely referred to as depressing or gloomy. It seems fitting that the arrival of Sun in the morning and its departure at night should so often provide the most majestic light shows on Earth—our reassuring daily miracle. Thank you, Sun!

The sun shines and warms and lights us and we have no curiousity to know why this is so; but we ask the reason of all evil, of pain, and hunger, and mosquitos and silly people.
—RALPH WALDO EMERSON

It was leftover materials from Sun's creation that assembled into Earth and the other planets. We are made from the solar afterbirth, so to speak, though it is not understood how this process was accomplished. Whether acting with intent or not solar forces would have been a prime agent in the conditioning of Earth over billions of years as it prepared for the arrival of multi-celled organic life. The life we enjoy depends en-tirely upon the sustenance of Sun. Without its light there would be no organic life on Earth other than a few deeply frozen and dormant bacte-ria. Even life around deep-sea thermal vents would eventually cease, as the oceans froze solid. Does it not seem unlikely that such a generous en-abler and supporter of life would itself be just an inanimate unconscious accident of the cosmos?

The dramatic proposition that prompted the writing of this book runs counter to everything that we, and many generations before us, have been taught and brought up to believe. It was fundamentally *not* a part of the scientific mindset in the 18th, 19th or 20th century, and is something that we dismissively reject from prior cultures as a symp-tom of their ignorance and lack of understanding. It is not a new prop-osition and, indeed, once held sway with the majority of this planet's population. It is not a threatening proposition, although millions of people and many entire cultures have been destroyed for supporting it. It is not a difficult proposition, although very little in the scientific, cultural or religious underpinnings of today's civilization even hints at it. And though it is not based on hard science there is nothing in hard or theoretical science that disproves the proposition.

The proposition is that Sun is a living, conscious being with an intelligence that dwarfs our own. I am not only suggesting that Sun is a large complex system with some form of self-governing intelligence to it, but also that it is a living being, aware of its self and its place in the Universe; that it is fully conscious and communicates with other conscious beings at its own level, and other levels; that its consciousness is so far beyond what we enjoy that it could be accorded deity status of a high order, and be recognized as a conscious being by atheists and agnostics, whatever spin they put on it.

As staggering as this proposition might seem, it is hardly novel, and was once held as a near universal belief or understanding in most parts of the globe. It is possible that generations of Neolithic peoples, the ancient Sumerians, Chaldeans, and Assyrians, the Egyptians, Greeks, Romans, Maya, Inca, Aztec, and the ancient Celts and Native Americans were not completely deluded. Perhaps they were right to regard Sun as a living celestial being, rather than view the prime enabler of life-on-Earth as just another random event in the infinity of space, deserving neither credit nor appreciation. We can add the world's 750 million Hindus to the list above, as well as followers of Shinto, the native Japanese religion revering Sun goddess Amaterasu.

Behold, my friends, the spring is come; the earth
has gladly received the embraces of the sun,
and we shall soon see the results of their love!
—SITTING BULL, SIOUX CHIEF

Whether Assyrian or Aztec, Celtic or Cherokee, priests in the cultures of Sun worship were capable of controlling and defining the religious arena as much as were the priests and their counterparts in the religions that replaced them. The Aztec hierarchy was capable of as much cruelty, greed, corruption, and deceit as the Christian zealots who slaughtered them in another god's name. Unfortunate stuff can and usually does happen when access to any god or spiritual truth is controlled by a priest-class and becomes defined by creed and dogma backed by scripture and authority.

Many have sought to explain how ancient cultures had knowledge of astronomical phenomena that were discovered by science in relatively recent times with cutting-edge equipment. We still struggle to explain the technology that was able to design and precision-build by hand the massive monuments and temples located in Egypt, Central America, China, Cambodia, Britain, and other parts of the world. Though various theories may exist as to building techniques and the nature of ceremonial activities, it is abundantly clear that early cultures held solar and celestial activities to be of far greater importance than does today's predominant culture.

The implications of a conscious solar entity are truly awesome, and might help to explain the "why" if not the "how" of some of the phenomena in the Solar System which astronomers view as strange but accidental coincidence. The most familiar of these to us will be that of the total solar eclipse. This spectacular event, giving a unique view of Sun's corona at specific times and places, arises from one of these strange coincidences. This is that Sun is exactly 400 times the diameter of the moon and is also 400 times as far away from Earth as the moon. It is this proportion that makes the full moon appear to be the same size as Sun in the sky, and because of this, when the moon slips exactly across the Sun's face, it perfectly eclipses it.

The entire miracle of our existence relies upon an extraordinary chain of coincidence that starts with the precise expansion rate of the Universe. From the birth of Earth, the single largest influence upon the links leading from then to now will have arisen from Solar influences. The effect that Sun has upon our planet is undoubtedly more complex than we

STEPHAN SEIP

can ever measure through calculating the pull of its gravity, the amount of radiation received per square centimeter per day, and information gleaned from other data-collecting exercises. Perhaps, too, the existence of this planet and the life forms upon it provides some value to the star that hosts us.

When looking at inspirational images that seek to depict gOd, the divine presence or spiritual truths you will notice that many of them incorporate depictions of Sun and its glorious rays of light, often obscured by cloud or horizon. It is little wonder why. The glorious and reassuring image of Sun is deeply ingrained in our mental image banks because, deep down, we have always recognized it to be the single most important factor in our lives.

A subconscious recognition of Sun as a conscious being survives today in popular culture, if the abundance of sunburst designs and smiley Sun faces is anything to go by. And once you look for solar imagery in graphics and design, it becomes inescapable. You will probably notice more of it from now on.

Our Sun has been around for over 4.5 billion years, about a third of the lifespan of the Universe. It is theorized that the planets assembled around Sun within its first 100 million years. And even though they are sitting on the evidence, so to speak, astro-physicists are still at a loss to explain just how Earth and her companion planets formed. However these diverse bodies of matter came to be, it is generally accepted that their source material came from the leftovers of the cloud of cosmic dust that gave birth to Sun.

After they formed, all the planets ended up with stable orbits, neither getting sucked into the Sun, nor spinning further distant. Pretty amazing, is it not? Ask a NASA scientist just how much work, calculation, and intention is required to successfully launch a satellite into orbit around this planet. Your average rocket scientist would be happy to achieve a stable orbit of 100 years, let alone the more than 4 billion years that Earth has been orbiting its Sun. Rocket scientists are able to assess a satellite's orbit after its launch and send out corrective adjustments over the years should it start to lose its stability. Could the Sun and its planets employ some subtle mechanism that achieves the same result?

The sun, with all those planets revolving around it and dependent on it, can still ripen a bunch of grapes as if it had nothing else in the universe to do.
—GALILEO GALILEI

The scientific explanation cannot consider that Sun had any conscious connection with the planets' formation or with the stability of their orbits. The concept of solar consciousness is so far outside the orthodox mindset that everything done by Sun is regarded as the sort of freak occurrence that can happen when a lot of atoms hang around for long enough in space. Even though Sun generates a stable and unimaginably powerful electromagnetic field that embraces the entire solar system, scientists appear not to have considered that this may play a role in the maintenance of the planets. This sort of activity would imply conscious management taking place (as do, of course, so many of Sun's other distinct activities).

Sadly, many people consider Sun to be little more than a convenient and steady source of natural illumination—our giant light bulb in the sky. As you will discover, Sun is a massive multi-levelled powerhouse with regular patterns to its activities, patterns that scientists are, as yet, unable to explain or understand. Sun is the source of complex and powerful forces that extend throughout the solar system, and has certainly got more going on inside it than does a rock or a power station. Sun has complexity and an array of self-generated activities that we would, in most circumstances, associate with an intelligent being. It is a well-designed complex organism of enormous proportions, with a huge electromagnetic presence.

Sun figures large in the solar system. If the combined mass of all the contents of the solar system were 1,000 kilograms, then 998 of them would be Sun, with Jupiter and Saturn containing most of the remaining two kilograms. Our little planet weighs in at just 100 grams. Heavyweight though it is, 98 percent of the Sun's content is made up of the two lightest elements in the Universe, hydrogen and helium—about three quarters and one quarter respectively.[12]

We'll now take a cruise through the seven different layers of Sun (they certainly did not know this much about it when your author was in school). You do not need to absorb all the detail of this information in order to digest the message of this book—but the spawning ground of light itself is an amazing place. And without it we clearly would not be here.

The study of solar activity will always be theoretical and based upon scientific efforts to make sense of the information gathered. There may be an alternative to today's standard model of the Sun's mechanisms that also fits the data at hand. And, of course, we can only discover those phenomena that we are able to detect. Before we knew of radio waves or magnetism, it is unlikely we would have been able to recognize these features of Sun.

There may yet be solar activities, strong or subtle, which are beyond our current technology of detection, or framework of understanding. And solar science is quite possibly studying no more than the side effects of what is really going on. It is as if technicians in a lab somewhere were reading sensors attached to a person playing in Wimbledon, getting data on their respiration, heartbeat, metabolism, grunting, and whatever. As they try to correlate the data and look at connections between the respiration and metabolism, the grunting and the heartbeat, they might well be completely unaware that a game of tennis is taking place.

THE SOLAR INTERIOR

We call that part of Sun that is visible to us the *interior,* its radius extending 700,000 kilometers from the core to the photosphere. The outer invisible layers constitute the *exterior,* extending 2 to 3 million kilometers into space. But Sun is not a solid body like Earth, and there is no edge or defined hard surface to it.

When the Solar and Heliospheric Observatory (SOHO) spacecraft went into orbit in 1995, we knew little of the complex activity taking place within Sun's interior. We cannot see through its opaque surface and it is too hot for us to send probes inside to check things out. SOHO changed all that when it revealed that the Sun's surface ripples like an agitated pond, and allowed scientists for the first time to hear the accompanying chorus of sounds. Though we cannot see into the Sun, we are able to listen into it. The vibrations reaching Sun's surface provide the information that enables helioseismologists to recognize the processes taking place within its four inner layers. We must take our hats off to these ingenious scientists.

In common with 99 percent of the Universe's other content, Sun's matter exists in the fourth state of matter called *plasma,* which is not solid, liquid, or gas. We are so familiar with our stable Earth-bound world of solids, liquids, and gasses that we can easily forget how unusual this kind of stuff is in the greater scheme of things. We are the exception. In plasma worlds, there does not exist the harmonious balance between positive and negative particles that we associate with atoms of stable matter. Therefore matter in a plasma state is charged and highly conductive of electromagnetic energy. Within plasma, particles move around freely as a fluid, even though they may be compressed to well beyond the density of the most solid matter we find on Earth. The most common natural examples we witness on this planet occur when air in the atmosphere assumes a plasma state and enables phenomena like lightning and the aurora borealis to occur.

The power source of the Sun originates in its core, extending out 175,000 kilometers from the center. Here, the plasma matter is at its most compressed, to almost eight times the density of gold. It is fiercely hot in there, at 15 million degrees Kelvin,[13] and in the intense heat and pressure the nuclei of hydrogen atoms fuse together, becoming helium nuclei and losing less than 1 percent of their mass in the process. In each and every second of this nuclear fusion reaction, that fraction of a percent equates to 4 million tons of Sun's mass converting from matter into energy, according to Einstein's famous formula $E = mc^2$. That's a lot of energy.

Sun's fundamental energy starts life as photons—particles of pure energy that emerge from the core in the form of high-energy gamma rays that would quickly turn us to toast. Fortunately, by the time they escape from Sun's surface, the photons have been processed into the safe visible light that facilitates life on Earth. Scientists calculate that Sun releases enough power in 1 second to meet the energy needs of the United States for 4 million years! You don't need to be a scientist to feel that blast of energy on a clear sunny day—coming through 150 million kilometers of space before it reaches us.

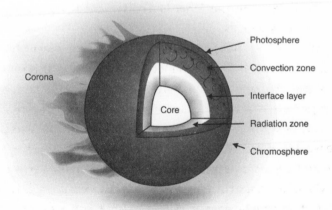

There is more than enough power in the explosive core of the Sun to blow apart our solar system. But it is contained by a 315,000 kilometer layer of plasma, which is 25 times as thick as Earth's diameter, having the density of gold where it surrounds the core. It is the *radiative zone,* and the newborn photons have to work their way through this layer on their journey outwards. They are travelling at the speed of light and, as the crow flies, this journey would take them just over 1 second. But it can take a million years or so for them to travel through the dense plasma, passing their energy from atom to atom on the way. Who knows what is going on during their journey through this incredibly thick soup of energy and matter? When they finally graduate from the radiative zone, nearly all of them will be vibrating within the safe spectrum of visible light—a range that is but a small portion of the full spectrum that energy can assume.

The radiative zone is rotating rigidly, like a solid object, with the core at its center. The next big layer beyond it, the *convection zone,* rotates around it—spinning at different speeds. In recent years solar scientists have detected a new region of Sun between these two zones, named the *interface layer,* or tachocline, which is generating more than just excitement in solar astronomy circles. It is suspected that, as the two giant zones surrounding it rotate at different speeds, they become a giant magnetic dynamo generating the energy that fuels Sun's powerful, mysterious and very active magnetic field. The invisible magnetic field of Sun is recognized as the source of most solar activity and is the least understood aspect of Sun. The interface layer has been described as being composed of giant twisting ropes of electromagnetic energy. Isn't it just amazing what matter is able to do, when there is enough of it in the mix?

The convection zone rises a further 200,000 kilometers, almost to the surface of Sun. At this point the density of Sun's matter has dropped from that of gold, to that of water. Not only does this level spin at a different speed from those underneath, it also rotates at different speeds around its own circumference. At its equator it makes a full rotation every 25 days, with the polar regions taking 35 days, although logic would expect the shorter polar rotation to take less time. Of course "logic," in the normal sense of the word, has already gone out the window.

Within the convective zone, the density and temperature have dropped sufficiently for some atoms to latch onto electrons and move from plasma to a more turgid gas state. Now the energy coming in from below is swiftly moved upwards as the matter heats, pushing up giant bubbles of energy-filled gas that measure thousands of kilometers across. They rise with a fractal turbulence, breaking into ever-smaller bubbles called granules. Near the surface the smaller granules flip over, releasing their energy load before dropping back to the bottom. Can you imagine this colossal ocean of hydrogen and helium gases seething like a boiling kettle—saturated with concentrated photon energy ready to burst forth into the galaxy? We will wait just a week for the charged photons to make their way through this ordered turbulence, finally reaching the visible outer edge of Sun as pure white light.

As Sun passes behind a thin cloud or sets below the horizon, the clear round outer edge that we see is the *photosphere*. The temperature has dropped down to a relatively cool 5,800 degrees Kelvin now, compared to the 15 million degree reactor at the center. It is relatively as thick as an onion skin (100 to 300 kilometers) with a density thinner by far than this planet's outer atmosphere. Yet, as is the case with all parts of Sun, there is a lot going on within this thin surface.

Sunspots on the photosphere were first studied by Galileo in 1610 and continue to excite great interest among solar scientists, due to their apparent though elusive connection with many other changing features of solar activity and phenomenon on Earth.

The photosphere's temperature drops up to 2,000 degrees Kelvin within sunspots, which are characterized by the presence of powerful magnetic fields. In size they can range from 15,000 to 50,000 kilometers across—large enough to line up four Earths end-to-end. Astronomers believe that sunspots are linked to meteorological phenomenon on Earth, including a mini ice age that paralyzed Northern Europe at the end of the 17th century.

The photosphere is the photons' last terminal as they complete a million years of maturation and embark upon their journey through the infinity of space, most of them never to encounter anything other than other photons on their trip across the Universe. Most of those that reach and interact with planet Earth will be absorbed as energy, but enough will bounce off to carry an image of our planet with them as they travel back into the darkness of space.

THE OUTER LEVELS: CHROMOSPHERE AND CORONA

Matter content is so thin in the outer layers of Sun that they are invisible to us, drowned out by the light shining from the photosphere. Fleetingly, these layers may be glimpsed only during the totality of a solar eclipse. We could reasonably expect the atmosphere of Sun to be a peaceful place, but it is far from calm up there. It is full of mind-bending riddles for solar astronomers, who understand more about what is going on inside Sun than they do about what takes place in its electrically charged, invisible outer levels.

The *chromosphere* is a ruby-red, jagged, and irregular region of the Sun, which is briefly visible to the eye during the seconds just preceding and following the totality of a solar eclipse. First spotted in 1851, it extends about 2,000 to 3,000 kilometers above the photosphere, and appears to be populated by long thin needles of red light. They are called *spicules*, measuring 500 to 1,000 kilometers across, and congregate by the thousands, rising rapidly to heights of several thousand kilometers. Believed to be driven by the acoustic vibrations of the photosphere, they live for less than 15 minutes, with most of them dissipating at their peak, and some of them dropping back to Sun's surface.

The entire chromosphere is covered with a sprawling network of interlinked magnetic field lines. In especially active areas huge numbers of these field lines congregate together in massed looping tangles. There is still great uncertainty over just what a spicule is, what the mysterious organization of magnetic fields achieves and how it is all created and maintained—let alone why. It would be presumptuous of me to speculate that this layer serves as Sun's receiving station for incoming information, but I do not doubt that the spicules and magnetic fields serve practical solar purposes. By the time we have traveled to the outer reaches of the chromosphere, just a few thousand kilometers from Sun's surface, the temperature has inexplicably increased nearly tenfold, from 5,800 to 20,000 degrees Kelvin.

Surrounding the irregularly shaped chromosphere is a little understood area of Sun known as the *transition region*. In this thin area, with a depth of approximately 150 kilometers, the temperature of the atmosphere leaps once again, this time from 20,000 to around 1 million degrees Kelvin. The region emits short-wavelength ultraviolet light that cannot penetrate Earth's atmosphere, and astronomers have only been able to view it since the advent of space-based imaging tools. To date, very little is known about what the transition region is or what it does, beyond being a cushion between the chromosphere and corona. If actually a layer of Sun, then there would be eight layers.

Now we reach the least understood feature of Sun and, perhaps, its crowning glory. The *corona*, occupying considerably more area in space than does Sun's physical "body," can stretch for 2 or 3 million kilometers beyond the photosphere. Temperatures have become hundreds of times hotter, ranging from 1 to 5 million degrees Kelvin. Why hasn't the heat emanating from Sun's surface just dissipated into the cold surrounding space? Where does this heat come from? Scientists struggle to understand.

The corona is essentially an invisible electromagnetic phenomenon, but the power of its activity and associated events are truly awesome. It only manifests to us during a 100 percent solar eclipse, since the tiniest fraction of Sun's light is enough to completely overwhelm that of its corona. What we see at this moment is its eponymous crown-like shape being outlined by the light released from free electrons streaming off the Sun and becoming excited by the corona's powerful magnetic field lines. Its shape is not constant, changing along with the sunspot cycle on the photosphere. Solar scientists can tell us very little about the corona itself, although it is held responsible for many other features of Sun's activity.

While scientists grapple with the very real difficulties of explaining the nature and existence of the Sun's corona, permit me to hypothesize about the possible relevance of this fascinating phenomenon. Perhaps the invisible corona is the most important feature of Sun—that to which all else is geared, and that which is responsible for some of its most far-reaching effects. It is difficult to resist the temptation to compare aspects of a living conscious Sun to our own existence, relating its fusion-reactor core to our own heart or its chromosphere full of spicules to our seeing apparatus. But it is, of course, a completely different nature of being and in some respects one might as well be looking for the nose of a cauliflower or the nipples of a trout.

It does seem reasonable, though, to look for the mind of a conscious Sun and here, perhaps, one need look no further than its corona. Like our own mind, the corona is an essentially invisible extension of Sun. As with the force lines of a magnet, all we can ever see is the effect of the corona upon particles that are in its presence.

Scientists continue to debate the very existence of a human mind—with some camps describing it as a mere illusion of the brain. This uncertainty will continue until tools are developed that are sensitive enough to register and measure the phenomenon of human consciousness and mind. In the perfect darkness of a total solar eclipse, does it not seem likely that we are witnessing the image of a mind infinitely more powerful than our own—without the need for special tools?

FRED ESPENAK

An intriguing spin-off from the corona is the *solar wind,* a stream of ionized gas (superheated electrons and free protons) that is accelerated

by the corona into an outward flow. This virtual extension of the corona becomes thinner and cooler as it blows off of Sun in all directions, meandering at speeds ranging from 300 kilometers a second to
900 kilometers a second as it extends its presence throughout the solar
system.

As the solar wind streams away from the rotating Sun, it twists into
a giant spiralling magnetic bubble, called the *heliosphere*, which reaches
out beyond Pluto to encompass our entire solar system in its protective
embrace. Eventually its particle content becomes too thin to overcome
gases in the interstellar region and it comes to a fairly abrupt end, called
the heliopause. This stable but charged and ever-changing solar wind is
simply described by those who study is as being very complicated, and
is sometimes viewed as an extension of Sun's corona. One must wonder
what the effect would be upon our family of planets were they not all
enclosed in this mysterious spiralling magnetic field?

As the solar wind passes by us, it shapes Earth's magnetic field into
a pear-like configuration. At the same time, Earth's field pulls many of
Sun's travelling electrons and protons into its atmosphere. When these
high-energy ions in the solar wind collide with molecules in the air at
Earth's poles they get excited and release photons into the sky. This generates the breathtaking aurora borealis—dancing full-color displays
called the northern lights and, in the southern hemisphere, the southern
lights, or aurora australis. One could almost imagine two related energy
fields celebrating their meeting with a party—or perhaps battling it out
for magnetic supremacy. The energy dancing through the skies at this
point is four times the total U.S. electricity consumption at the peak of
its air-conditioned summer demand.[14]

Whilst first searching online for a company that organized tours to
see the aurora borealis, the closest thing I could find was a Japanese tour
company offering trips to the Artic Circle for newlyweds. These young
lovers hoped to conceive a child while being impregnated with the solar
wind. Of course, these dancing lights in the sky could be some completely random electromagnetic occurrence with no relevance to anything else on this planet. But with a show like that taking place, one

has to suspect that some other function of relevance might be going on; some useful exchange taking place.

Connected somehow with sunspot activity, *coronal mass ejections* can happen anything from once a week to six times a day during solar maximum (here's one for those Japanese tourists). The corona is primarily a magnetic entity with very little matter content—by our standards it is almost a vacuum. In a mass ejection, a billion tons of Sun's highly charged plasma (a thin hot mix of free protons, electrons and other particles) slowly breaks loose from the corona and accelerates as it is blasted into space. If pointed in our direction, it could reach Earth in three days and occasionally does. This happened in 1989 when one zapped Quebec, knocking out the city's entire power system and its emergency backup. Damage is regularly inflicted upon sensitive equipment around the world and research is ongoing to try and predict ejections that are headed towards us. Why, what, how? More riddles.

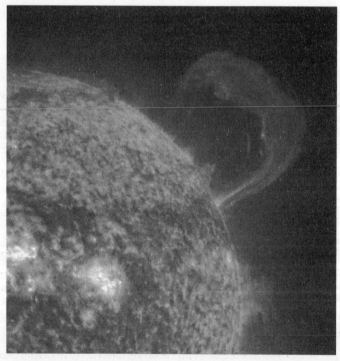

NASA/SOHO

Within the corona, long streaming *filaments* of cooler gas hang and loop, suspended by the ever-shifting magnetic field lines. They can be hundreds of thousands of miles long, and survive for days or weeks on end, slowly changing shape as they shift above Sun's chromosphere. Micro flares at their base send powerful acoustic waves through the filaments, generating cosmic "organ music" sound booms which can last for an hour before dissipating in the corona. Their eventual dissolution will sometimes trigger solar flares and coronal mass ejections. These filaments, also called *coronal prominences,* defy all logic and have been described as the equivalent of ice cubes surviving in a hot oven.

Imagine an explosion with more power than a million volcanoes that instantly hurtles a North American-sized chunk of Sun's surface into the air at speeds of many hundreds of kilometers per second. This can be the power of a single *solar flare,* another phenomenon considered to be controlled by the corona. During periods of sunspot activity, active regions of Sun can lose several flares a day for weeks on end. Astronomer Jack B. Zirker estimated that the energy contained in a single solar flare would power the United States for 40,000 years.

But perhaps we are missing the point by simply comparing one measure of energy to another. Whether we are generating energy in North America or Africa, Siberia or Singapore, things are being done with it, changed with it and achieved with it. We don't go to such lengths to generate power simply to produce firework displays. Is it unreasonable to consider that when Sun generates incredible amounts of energy and does various and specific things with it, there is also purpose and function—something being done?

Vast releases of electromagnetic energy accompany many of the solar processes above. This is then transmitted throughout the solar system and beyond to the surrounding galaxy. Solar flares are one such process, and radio astronomers have discovered how to listen to the radio signals that accompany them. They have categorized at least five different types of signal, with distinct characteristics to each, some of them displaying harmonics.

It is generally assumed that solar radio signals have no actual purpose, and simply represents meaningless emissions triggered by automatic primary processes, akin to the gas that escapes from us after a poorly di-gested meal. But perhaps the incredible capacity for communication that is available within Sun's electromagnetic exports is being put to active use. Who knows what sorts of conversations might take place between our Sun and other stars, or for what purpose they would exchange in-formation? But one could be excused for thinking that that looks like what is going on.

I often wonder how a solar scientist, intimately familiar with the pro-cesses taking place, can avow with a straight face that the coordinated complex activities of this celestial organism can be explained by acciden-tal, mechanical, and unmanaged process? It may not be that Sun directly controls things like its internal fusion engine, or the processes taking place in its radiative and convective zones—any more than we directly control the automatic processes of heartbeat, digestion or breathing. But it is difficult to escape the conclusion that Sun does have conscious man-agement of many other features, particularly those which most solar sci-entists believe to be controlled by its corona.

If we were to sum up the total computing power in place on this planet, it would probably rate as a drop of water to the ocean when com-pared to the potential processing power of Sun. But such comparisons are frivolous for Sun is no more a computer than you or I. It is a self-organized conscious being—something quite different.

Sun, though but one of many stars in this galaxy, is the most appro-priate candidate there can be for a prime divinity, not to mention the blindingly obvious one. Sun is right there, in our face—no faith required and needing no special rules to guide us to the light. It was always the instinctive choice. Sunlight and bliss—why do the words go so well to-gether? Do we really need all those allegorical references to the light of some invisible and intangible gOd of scripture and revelation and regu-lar redefinition? The ineffable inner light of spiritual connection may or may not be dependent on solar energies, but without Sun we would not be connected to it.

Sun is with us every day—closer and more accessible than the ped-dlers of modern religion would ever have us believe. I just believe that if we are to be expressing gratitude for our existence, as humans are inclined to do at times, then we might as well direct some of it at a deserving recipient. It's always nice to be appreciated, though Sun will probably get on with whatever its existence is all about, as it has done for nearly 4.5 billion years, with or without the appreciation of human beings.

Say hello...back
getting in touch

THE WHOLE IDEA of any communication with Sun or, heaven forbid, reverence towards it comes through our cultural filter as something dark and dangerous at worst, or ignorant and primitive at best. This is somewhat ironic, but it is not surprising considering that most impressions we have of solar worship are those reported by the same priests who burned or melted down everything they could find that was connected to it.

So how do we get in touch with our Sun? There are not a lot of precedents in a culture that has for countless generations looked down to the ground in prayer and denied the status of conscious being to our own prime provider of life. Whatever ancient cultures thought about Sun has been destroyed, lost, or locked away in the vaults of the Vatican. But all lost knowledge originated in the minds of humans and remains, in theory, retrievable or replaceable. Nothing can be more natural than to enjoy the feel of Sunshine on our face and body—to soak up its goodness.

What can you do now, though, without reference to doctrines or trained intermediaries or learned priests, if you wish to create a connection to the life-giving Sun? First, let go of 2 thousand years of Old Testament brainwashing and open your mind to the understanding that this ball of light in the sky that brings us life is itself a living thing. With eyes closed, face towards the Sun raising your head to spread its rays evenly across cheeks and forehead. Feel the light flooding into your closed eyelids and the rest of your face as it warms your skin from far away. Feel the silent rays of Sun as they feel you. And say hello . . . back.

*Turn your face to the sun
and the shadows fall behind you.*
—MAORI PROVERB

This can be a silent exchange and is one drawing purely on innate skills that are accessible to all, needing neither ritual nor apparatus. There are no rules on how to appreciate the rays of Sun. It feels good because it is good. Engage with the experience and listen to what comes to mind. Breath deeply, inhaling the energy. Direct the rays into ailing parts of your body. And just be with it, without thought, being the experience and the light. We do not need anybody to help us interpret the feel of Sunlight on our skin or to tell us that it brings warmth and light into this world.

It is enriching to capture those moments when we can safely look directly at Sun, in all its glory. This is one of the special features of the setting Sun, when the blinding glare usually becomes a defined and viewable red and yellow orb as Sun readies to slip beneath the horizon. I once revelled in half an hour of Sunrise at a Smallworld festival in Kent, watching as it slowly rose through a fine Arthurian mist that imbued Sun with the quality of a glowing full moon. Sometimes we can safely watch Sun obscured by thin clouds or reflected off water and glass. But always take care, as looking directly at a fully radiant Sun can cause eye damage. Your instincts should guide you, but always be cautious. Even if you think it looks perfectly safe, take a quick passing glance first and then look away. There should be no phantom spot in your vision if Sun is sufficiently dimmed.

There will be countless means for saying "hi" or for paying our respect to this greatest provider and maintainer of life energy. At another extreme from the simple technique above is the classic yoga Sun Salutation, which combines body movement with awareness so as to absorb the maximum of beneficial energies from the rising Sun. Hindus have long venerated a living bliss-dispensing Sun and this understanding is expressed and focused in their salutation. Using recognized forms has the advantage of benefiting from the experience of others and facilitating activity in a group, which can add further power to the experience.

I think you might dispense with half your doctors
if you would only consult Dr. Sun more.
—HENRY WARD BEECHER

The "Say Hello...Back" approach is simply an easy way to make the connection and is something that anybody can achieve. Recognizing that our Sun is not a lump of unconscious accident is the first step from which all else will follow. There is no need to wait for special opportunities to "get in touch." Sun does not need its special day of the week; it's there every one of them, even if the weather is between us, and we need no purpose-built building to get in touch. We have everything we need.

Far away in the sunshine are my highest aspirations.
I may not reach them, but I can look up
and see their beauty, believe in them,
and try to follow where they lead.
—LOUISA MAY ALCOTT

The solar system
our closest family in the cosmos

MUCH DEBATE has been devoted to the possibility and probability of there being organic life on other planets, in other star systems. Let us look at it another way. Imagine that you lived all your life in a remote community beside a large and isolated lake that provided a rich source of fish to your diet. You have never traveled beyond the area and, indeed, have no knowledge whatsoever about the rest of the planet. One day you send up a camera on a balloon and discover that there are other lakes dotted across the planet, and the nearest one is 1,000 kilometers away. Would you be surprised to one day discover that some of them also contained fish?

It seems reasonable to suppose that if our own star, Sun, is able to have a planetary system around it, then it is also possible that other stars in this Universe may have the same—and probable that many do. Yet until the early 1990s, the scientific status quo relegated any notion of other solar systems (with or without life) to the category of science fiction. The creation of our own planets seemed so unlikely an occurrence to astronomers that they could not conceive of it ever having accidentally happened elsewhere. However, a few of them risked ridicule and "sent up a balloon" anyway.

In 1995, the planetary searchers detected their first planet orbiting Pegasus 51, a star 40 light years away (300 trillion miles). The "giveaway" is a wobble in its rotation that is consistent with the gravitational effect of a very large gas planet, such as Jupiter, in a relatively fast and close orbit. The numbers of giant gas planets detected now run into the hundreds and the search has begun for smaller solid planets. When astronomers eventually find something more closely resembling Earth, the debate will open once again as to whether intelligent beings, or fish, exist anywhere else in Universe.

Believed to have originated from the solar afterbirth, the cloud from which the planets were born contained all the atoms of all the elements that were to form the basis of these new worlds. It is safe to assume that without our Sun none of these planets would be hanging out in this patch of the galaxy—none of them would even be. Whether the other planets were created by chance events, Sun, a Biblical gOd, or something else, we cannot assume that because only one of them is of any use to us, all of the rest are dead and purposeless phenomena.

There was a time before TVs and telephones, before cafes and cinemas, before newspapers and books—a time when the most exciting (and just about the only) visual entertainment in the evening was to be had by gazing at the heavens. People spent a lot of time watching the stars and the motions of the planets, often obscured to us by today's proliferating light-pollution. They spent a lot of time thinking about them too, far more than would the average person today. I suspect that more people then were able to pick out the planets in the night sky, aware that they move in an irregular path and that, unlike stars, they do not twinkle.

Without telescopes or means to measure the size and distance of astronomical objects, it was known that Jupiter was the king of the planets, even though the much-smaller Venus often appears larger and brighter. Were they able to somehow "feel" aspects of the planets from the vibrations being received with the light, using senses that we have forgotten how to employ? They also described planetary personalities, which may have been sensed through those same light vibrations.

It was, perhaps, the intuitively arising belief that astronomical events had an influence upon our lives that led our distant ancestors to develop the science of astrology in the first place. Our moon and each of the planets was perceived to have particular qualities, to have a character of its own and this character was commonly believed to have an influence upon our lives. The position and movement of these bodies was carefully studied and tracked and integrated into the "system" that is our existence. Now that we are aware of the difference that a butterfly's wing flap can have upon an entire weather system, is it so silly to suggest that a developing fetus could be affected by the positions of nearby planets, not to mention the ocean-lifting pull of the moon and the orbit-powering pull of Sun?

Of the eight planets other than Earth, five are visible to the naked eye. Together with the moon and Sun, they gave their names to the seven days of the week in Sanskrit, Latin, and most European languages.

Monday: Moon day, *lundi* in French for *luna* (moon)
Tuesday: Mars, *mardi* in French; *Tiwes-deg* after the Anglo-Saxon god of war, *Tiw*
Wednesday: Mercury, *mercredi* in French
Thursday: Jupiter, Norse god of thunder *Thor* (Thor's day)
Friday: Venus, *vendredi* in French; Norse equivalent *Freya*
Saturday: Saturn
Sunday: Sun

Earth did not have a day in its week.

This chapter takes us on a spin through the solar neighborhood and its main residents—a mixed and interesting bunch of characters. Much of what we understand and theorize about other planets grows and changes with each new mission into space. If you do not find this to be of interest then you may jump to the next chapter without fear of losing the plot.

With the possible exception of Venus, each of the planets in our solar system possesses its own unique electromagnetic field, which is in constant interaction with the solar wind. Many of the planets are thought to have hot centers, although, understandably, we know even less about them than we do about the core of our own planet. Each one of the planets is different from the others, possessing unique characteristics and features. Even more strange variety can be found in the more than one hundred and fifty moons and satellites that orbit the other planets.

Mercury is the closest planet to Sun, travelling around it faster than all the others, much like the winged messenger god from which it gets its name. Scientists at NASA were surprised to discover a complex magnetic field surrounding Mercury when their Messenger spacecraft made its first flyby in 2008. The flyby also revealed a complex and highly active exosphere. Mercury is small, a little bigger than our moon, and is the second densest planet in the solar system after Earth. Its orbit is more elliptical than other planets, swinging it so far away from Sun that it experiences the greatest differences between winter and summer temperatures of any planet. Mercury's surface has lots of variety, with smooth plains, mountains, volcanoes, craters and a polar region showing signs of frozen water.

Venus, usually the brightest object in the night sky after the moon, orbits between Mercury and Earth. Its atmosphere is so covered in thick layers of cloud that most of what we know about the landscape comes from imaging radar pictures. These show rolling plains with some mountains and many thousands of volcanoes, as well as frequent lightning. Venus is only slightly smaller than our planet but has much more land surface since there are no oceans. It seems to have a fairly similar composition and structure to Earth, which is why it was long suspected of harboring pointy-eared Venusians. However, the pressure at the surface of Venus is equivalent to being 1 kilometer below the ocean (90 atmospheres) and the 470 degree Centigrade heat at its surface would melt lead piping. Venus spins so slowly on its axis that it will orbit all the way around Sun and a bit (taking 243 Earth days), before its day is complete—before there have been two Sunsets. Every day would have to be your birthday in a situation like that.

Until Copernicus came along in the late 16th century, most of us believed that Earth was the center and prime focus of the Universe, instead of another planet orbiting Sun. The water abundance of Earth, covering almost 70 percent of its surface with liquid oceans and seas, is unique to the solar system, yet just a few percent of its watery realms have been explored.

We know more about our oceans, though, than we do about that what lies just beneath the crust of our own planet. The theories we have are scientific conjecture based primarily on the results of seismic probing —the only "hard" evidence comes up in lava flows bursting through the upper mantles, and this molten rock originates from just 50-200 kilometers below the surface. The core is another 3,000-5,000 kilometers down. Nobody has drilled very far towards it yet—there just aren't the tools. Traditionally, Earth's core is thought to be composed of molten iron about 2,500 kilometers in diameter. A favorite new theory considers it to be hot pressurized iron in crystal form, surrounded by molten lava. In 1692 the astronomer Edmund Halley believed the center of Earth to be hollow and inhabited, with escaping gas responsible for the aurora borealis. Geophysicist Marvin Herdon believes there to be a nuclear reactor generating heat in the heart of the planet. We may never be sure of just what is really down there.

We know a little more about the hard crust of Earth on which we live. Its thin skin is made up of giant slabs, called plates, which drift around independently of the hot mantle below—shaking us up occasionally as they do. Silicon, the basis of quartz crystal, is the second most abundant element in Earth's crust, after oxygen. And yes, Earth is probably the only planet supporting complex organic life-as-we-know-it in this stellar system. Many of our pre-Christian ancestors recognized that the planet sustaining our existence was itself an entity, and granted it goddess status. In Greece her name was Gaia, and the most binding oaths were those sworn in her name. In Gnostic times, her name was Sophia.

The fourth planet from Sun is Mars. Though much smaller than Earth, it has about the same area of land surface, since none is taken up by oceans. When not obscured by clouds the landscape is both varied and spectacular. Little Mars claims the biggest mountain in the whole solar system, Olympus Mons. Resting in the plains, the base of this megamountain measures 500 kilometers in diameter. Its peak is a lofty 24 kilometers (14 miles) from its bottom—almost three times the height of Mt. Everest. Mars retains an enormous scar from the monster meteorite that long ago carved a crater 2,000 kilometers wide and 6 kilometers deep on its surface.

Mars was for many years thought to be the most likely of the other planets to sport human-like life, always assumed to have skin that was green in color. In part, this reputation arose because of images that appear to be the dried-up beds of rivers, lakes and canals—indicating that Mars may have once contained life-supporting water, and life that was intelligent enough to channel it into straight lines. Now it is dry and hot, with tornado-like red-dust twisters 1 kilometer wide and 10 kilometers high that roam the planet hurling out lightning bolts as they go. Mars is the outermost of the solid planets.

At 1,300 times the volume of Earth, gas-giant Jupiter is a hive of electromagnetic energy, with parts of its powerful magnetic field reaching 650 million kilometers into space, beyond the orbit of neighboring Saturn. High-energy particles are ejected from its magnetosphere, some of them even reaching so far that they come into Earth's orbit. Jupiter radiates more energy into space than it receives from Sun, and could be seen as a closer relative to Sun than Earth, being constructed primarily of the same two elements, hydrogen and helium. For all we know, Jupiter might be an even more important and valued member of this solar family than is Earth.

We are spirit attached to an organic body. Who knows what manner and variety of spirit exists within the gigantic electromagnetic gas ball that is king of the planets, with its multilayered active swirling atmosphere, stable bands, spots, and more than sixty orbiting moons? Both the Pioneer and Voyager missions measured exchanges of electrical current between Jupiter and its larger moons. The current was most pronounced between Io and Jupiter, at 5 million amperes with a power of 2,500 billion watts (that's 3.3 billion horsepower) flowing through what looks like an "umbilical cord" between the moon and the planet. It is the cause of giant dancing auroras at Jupiter's poles, which may be thousands of times brighter than Earth's auroras. What is going on here—whatever principles are at play, how is it that matter floating in space comes together to make structures that are as organized and complex as Jupiter?

Saturn is placed sixth from Sun, and is by far the largest planet after Jupiter. It was known from prehistoric times, although its rings were not discovered and described until the 17th century. Fainter and darker rings have also been discovered on Neptune, Uranus, and Jupiter since the late 1970s. Multiple moons and rings seem to be a hallmark of gas planets. The rings of Saturn are complicated, being composed of hundreds of grouped ringlets, each made up of small pieces of ice and rock in independent orbits. The rings are only about a kilometer thick but extend a quarter million or more kilometers into space. The outermost ring is a system of combined rings with complex interactions. Sometimes the rings develop a radial structure causing strange spokes to appear that survive for hours or days. It is thought that Saturn's strong electromagnetic field causes these patterns.

Astronomers perceive that Saturn's ring system is crucially managed by three of its moons: Atlas, Pandora, and Prometheus, which are called the "shepherding satellites." More than fifty other moons have been identified around Saturn, an increase on the twenty-seven known when I began writing this book. Many of these moons are co-ordinated with each other and maintain synchronous rotations, appearing to somehow be scheduling their orbits. Saturn possesses an unusual luminosity that astronomers have yet to explain. Funny old matter.

Uranus, the third largest planet, was discovered in such modern times that we actually know who first identified it—William Herschel, through his telescope, on March 13, 1781. It is icy and covered in clouds. Like the other gas planets, it has a veritable harem of moons, with five big ones and more than twenty smaller ones. In recent times, astronomers have been able to detect eleven fainter Saturn-style rings complementing Uranus' moons. A curious thing about Uranus is that it does not spin with its central equatorial regions towards Sun. Its spin has the north and south pole getting the more direct Sun.[15] Notwithstanding this, astronomers are puzzled by the fact that it is nevertheless warmer at the equator and they are still arguing the toss over which of its poles is north and which south.

Neptune was predicted before it was even discovered. This was because of the gravitational effect it was having upon the orbit of the newly discovered Uranus. It was then first spotted in 1846 and a dispute broke out between England and France over who discovered it. It boasts the fastest winds in the solar system, reaching up to 2,500 kilometers per hour as giant storms of hydrogen, helium, and methane sweep through the atmosphere. One of its eight moons, Triton, is notable for being the only moon in the solar system that orbits in the opposite direction to its planet's rotation. Neptune has four rings, one with a curious twisted shape and its outermost one in three parts. Like Jupiter and Saturn, Neptune is thought to have a hot center, and radiates more energy out into the cosmos than it receives from our Sun.

The dwarf of the solar system, now demoted from its planetary status, Pluto is smaller than seven planetary moons, including Earth's. Regardless of changes made to its astronomical categorization, Pluto itself will no doubt continue to be whatever it is, traveling in an erratic orbit that sometimes pulls it closer to Sun than Neptune. Due to its great distance and small size, there is not a large amount known about Pluto.

The moons of the solar system have at least three hundred active volcanoes among them, some belching out torrents of icy slush instead of hot magma. The biggest lunar volcano of them all is Prometheus, on Jupiter's moon Io, and it is the most active volcano in the solar system, shooting gases more than 100 kilometers into space. Many of the moons support geysers spouting higher than any planetary ones, sometimes sending plumes of gas and dust as high as 8 kilometers into space. The variety among moons orbiting these planets shows more diversification than the planets themselves.

In between small solid Mars and gas giant Jupiter lies the asteroid belt. There are probably a million or more of these variously shaped lumps made of metal, solid rock, or aggregated bits of stuff. Though very occasionally they travel in pairs, or have their own mini-moons, there does not seem to be much happening between asteroids, other than lots of collisions. Nothing seems to be marshaling them, as with the rings and moons of the gas planets. Neither do all these smaller bits of matter join up into a bigger ball, as some suggest happened when the planets were formed. Perhaps this zone between the solid and the gas planets serves as some kind of a solar system scrap yard where drifting debris ends up.

Far less understood than asteroids are the mysterious comets, which have been invested with great import by sky-watching cultures through the ages. They are composed of materials extant at the very beginnings of the solar system, and were recently found to contain high levels of organic compounds—necessary ingredients for life. Some have even suggested that an interaction with comets was integral to the process that brought both water and life to Earth. They were often considered to be messages of some kind or portents of disaster.

It is believed that comets originate from distant regions of our solar system, including the Oort Cloud, a vast cloud of ice and dust well beyond the orbit of Pluto. There could be billions of comet-like objects, some of which occasionally break loose and travel through the solar system. Like Halley's and Hale-Bopp comets, most of these orbit Sun on predictable paths, with orbiting periods ranging from as little as seven years to several billion years. The warmth of Sun creates the visible tail of a comet, as ice within it vaporizes into gas and is carried off the comet's head by the solar wind. Whatever their purpose, comets will continue to fulfill it whether we understand it or not.

There are many books available to inform us about the different vibrational, spiritual, and astrological characteristics of the planets, as are there volumes on the different aspects of crystal and gemstones. Some of them are by scholars, some by mystics, and some by people with powerful imaginations. Delivering such information is not the remit of this chapter, which simply proposes that many of our fellow planets display the symptoms of being "joined-up" phenomena, which are playing some part in their own destiny and that of their immediate surroundings.

Perhaps the entire solar system is like some form of a garden, or maybe a family for Sun. Whatever their purpose, it is reasonable to suppose that both the existence and development of the planets has relevance and value to Sun. They are more than just accidental balls of matter travelling through space with no agenda. They are key players in our cohesive and complex solar system—the brothers and sisters of Mother Earth.

Nature does nothing uselessly.
—**ARISTOTLE** (384 – 322 B.C.)

Stars

is there content to the twinkle?

WHEN WE LOOK at a distant star we do not see it in the same way that we see most other objects in our world, like daffodils and mountains. We see things that are around us because light, whether from Sun, fire or an electric bulb, has struck them and bounced off again, carrying information about their properties. When we gaze at a star we are absorbing light directly from that which we see; light that was produced in a star system many trillions of miles away; light that has been absorbed as energy by our eye after years of travelling through time and space.

Although stars may vary more in physical proportions and characteristics than do we from the other primates, they all belong to a particular celestial family. Emanating from the same universal womb, they are primarily composed of hydrogen, from 20 to 30 percent helium, and up to 2 percent of other elements. The same type of nuclear fusion reaction powers them all, creating energy through the steady conversion of hydrogen to helium. But they are by no means all alike.

Stars are truly the transmutation machines of the cosmos, steadily converting their original hydrogen and helium atoms into most of the elements of the periodic table. In the immense pressure and heat of a star's interior, the simple original atoms of hydrogen and helium will be transmuted into more complicated atoms, with more neutrons and protons in the nucleus surrounded by up to 25 electrons circling in four different orbits. Though we don't really understand how the stars do it, the transmutation brings into existence all the elements from oxygen and carbon up to the light metals like chromium. This freshly fabricated matter may constitute up to 2 percent of the average star's mass.

If a star is large enough, it will complete its physical life with a giant supernova explosion. During this brief moment in the life of a giant star, enough light is emitted to outshine an entire galaxy, and only in the unimaginable force of that explosion are further elemental transformations made possible. This extraordinary environment enables the production of more complicated elements, including heavier metals such as iron, silver, gold, mercury, and uranium. After the blast, these newly created elements end up in clouds of inter-stellar dust, such as that which once condensed into Sun and its nine planets. All of Earth's hydrogen and some of its helium have been around since the very beginning, but every other element upon this planet was subsequently fashioned on a star. Ninety percent of the matter that makes up Earth was once part of a burning star.

Whilst the telescopic tools of astronomy have not been around for the million years it would take to witness the birth of a star, the Hubble telescope has photographed some of the different stages involved, and added flesh to theories of star formation. The process may take place in small clouds of interstellar dust holding enough matter to make up from one to a dozen stars. Or the clouds can be massive nebulae stretching from a hundred to over a thousand light years across. These cosmic nurseries act as wombs to hundreds of new stars, which ignite to illuminate the shape of the nebulae, fluorescing the gases within.

Long theorized, and now seen through Hubble, is star formation arising from the pressures and energies created when giant galaxies collide. At these times many millions of stars may come into being in one spectacular burst of creation.

Whether it is colliding galaxies, a nearby exploding supernova or gravity waves emanating from a galaxy's arms, a "disturbance" of some sort is believed to be the spark that initiates star formation. This disturbance is believed to, by some means, trigger the simple gas to condense into spinning disks that suck in more and more matter, accumulating heat as they do it. After about a million years, not very long in the life of the Universe, the center of this disk will reach the ferocious temperature necessary to switch on the fusion reaction that will power the new star for thousands of millions of years thereafter.

When this reaction kicks in, the baby star will have condensed into a ball that is just dense enough around the outer layers that when its center explodes with the power of a quadzillion hydrogen bombs, the blast will be contained. Its energy thereafter permeates the surrounding layers to eventually emerge as light. At this time it also somehow blasts away all the remaining interstellar dust, which thereafter has the potential to form planets, comets, and so on.

There are other hypotheses about the accidental process that is able to turn dust into stars, and there are other factors suspected of triggering the process. Astronomers think that many of them might be correct. There could be a variety of different techniques that lead to star conception—a veritable cosmic *Kama Sutra*.

Most of the theoretical explanations for star birth rely upon events that take place within the existing Universe to trigger the process. In the original Universe, of course, there were just thin dark clouds of gas and no apparent triggers. If we were looking for events that triggered the birth of humans, we could find many. These could include passionate love, drunken abandon, pounding lust, the desire for heirs or the want of a spouse. But they would all be just that—triggers for an event that is no accidental phenomenon, but a natural part of being human.

Stars come in different sizes, most of them ranging from one-tenth to ten times Sun's diameter. The smaller the star variety, the cooler they burn and the longer they live. We cannot see the most populous stars in our galaxy, small red dwarfs, since most of their photons emerge in infrared wavelengths instead of visible light. They will live for hundreds of billions of years, compared to the 5 or 10 billion years that Sun-sized stars survive. It looks like the meek will, at least, inherit the Universe.

The Universe's hottest stars are the blue giants, which exhaust their fuel supplies after a mere 10 million years or so. Their fierce cores burn at well over 100 times the temperature of Sun as they generate a magnetic field extending 14,000 times the distance of Sun's. It is the blue giants that will end their days in a supernova explosion. Once the fuel in a blue giant's core has been consumed, there is nothing resisting the massive gravitational pressure of the star's outer layers. These then collapse into the center of the star, triggering the spectacular supernova explosion that sends energy, physical remnants and newly forged elements out into space.

The remaining matter of the blue giant then collapses into one of the stranger characters of the Universe—a neutron star. Such objects have been detected in space, measuring a mere 20 to 30 kilometers in diameter. Their density is estimated to be several billion tons per cubic centimeter; a pea-sized piece of a neutron star would weigh more than the Titanic. How can such a density be possible? It is achievable because, in the ferocity of the supernova, the atoms are stripped of their electrons, which make up less than 1 percent of their mass while defining more than 99.99 percent of their volume.

The gravity pull of a neutron star is tremendous, acting like a super magnet to pull any passing matter into itself. When this small star reaches a certain mass, beyond three solar masses, it has such a gravitational pull that even light is unable to escape its attraction. At this point it has become the enigmatic black hole that has intrigued so many since its existence was predicted by Einstein's Theory of Relativity. In recent years, astronomers have claimed to see fairly convincing evidence of black holes, and believe a huge one rests in the center of most galaxies.

Whether red dwarf, Sun-sized, or blue giant, it seems apparent that every star in the Universe will manifest its own unique electromagnetic signature. Combined with this will also be a unique configuration of corona, stellar wind, spots, flares, and many of the phenomena we detect in our own star, plus others of which we are not yet aware. Though our language may not possess the words required to describe or define the character or nature of a star, "personality" would not be an inappropriate term.

Unlike the solitary Sun, from half to two-thirds of the stars out there are binary. They have a nearby partner called a companion star and are linked for life, some performing like a couple of pair-figure skaters and others simply spinning rapidly around each other. Astronomers are able

to determine the mass of stars by observing the behavior of the two orbits in a binary system. Some have suggested that Sun may once have
had a partner. Perhaps the predominant assumption that Sun represents
masculine qualities rests in our lack of a female star, considering that
qualities such as warmth and nurturing and comforting are all within
the female arena. So too is the provision of nourishment, which arises
from the original energy source of Sun's light.

We could easily assume that the hundreds of billions of stars living within a galaxy might be evenly or randomly distributed. But that
would be about as sensible as assuming that the one billion people living
in India were all evenly or randomly distributed around the country. In
fact, like us, stars live in stellar communities called clusters, with empty
space between them. There might be a dozen or so, a few hundred, a few
thousand, or a few million stars in these groupings, rather like we get
together in farms, villages, towns, and cities. It seems unlikely that stars
would have planning departments determining just where they can be,
but they do like to be in close proximity to other stars.

Astronomers are able to detect and measure the vibrating wave energies transmitted by stars and galaxies throughout the Universe. This is
done with all manner of high-tech equipment and lots of high-powered
thinking. But what are they doing with all this information, with these
electromagnetic broadcasts made by Sun and other stars?

It is as if some alien entities, that knew only telepathic communication, were to pick up and analyze a radio talk show broadcast from Earth.
Assuming they could listen to the radio they would probably convert
the sound wave patterns to graphic displays of the type we are familiar with. They might discover there were a number of different sources
(voices) of the sound waves and possibly even detect certain audio patterns (words) being repeated at different rates. They might measure the
lengths of pauses and breathing rate and all manner of associated and
related data. But they would, essentially, have no idea of what was being
said—perhaps not even realize that what they were analyzing represented an exchange of intelligence and information.

Galaxies
our brains are not unlike them

C ONSIDER, for a moment, that the galaxy in which we live might itself be structured to operate as one enormous entity, a single organism processing and responding to information on a cosmic scale. In the Milky Way's galactic processor each of its hundreds of billions of stars could be equivalent to a single neuron firing in our brains. Stars, as we have seen, are equipped to produce and dispatch vast and varied amounts of electro-magnetic energy into the cosmos. At the same time, they will be exposed to the energy outputs of thousands of other nearby stars. Our own manipulation of electromagnetic energy is fundamental to most of the data processing and communication technology we use on Earth. Yet astrophysicists generally assume that the complex and cumulative electromagnetic output of all the stars in a galaxy is just useless random noise.

Our brains contain neurons in the same orders of scale that apply to star population in galaxies—hundreds of billions. Nerve cells communicate by sending bioelectric messages to each other across synapses, jumping across the synapse gap at the end of their axons. A typical neuron might have ten-thousand synapse "connections" to other neurons, and be carrying on separate "conversations" with any number of them simultaneously. Each neuron is both an individual player and part of a big team with no clear manager.

Like stars, the brain's neurons come in various shapes and sizes, and nobody pretends to know much about them, or how they conspire to direct activity and enable thought processes. But we do know a lot more about them than we know about stars—enough, at least, to recognize that the signals neurons exchange are purposeful, although individually they might appear to be just random noise.

Perhaps this is one more example demonstrating the principle of scale and proportion—a pattern of similar structures appearing in smaller and larger harmonics of creation. According to Einstein's Theory of Relativity, you will travel light years in a twinkle if you are the light itself. As far as the photon is concerned it will get to its destination, whether on Earth or the other end of the galaxy, at the same moment it leaves the star on which it was created. What does this mean in a galaxy where each star is connected by a virtual cable of light to its neighbors, carrying the potential to exchange large amounts of data and information?

Coming back down to earth, galaxies are simply where the stars live, and the Milky Way is but one of hundreds of billions of galaxies. Until Edwin Hubble, in 1923, established that a cloud of gas in the Milky Way named M31 was, in fact, a far distant galaxy, we had assumed that all the stars in the night sky represented the entire Universe. We now recognize that all of the stars we see live within this galaxy and that for every one visible to the naked eye, there are tens of millions that are not. Ours is a disc-shaped spiralling galaxy that is about 100,000 light years across and 1,000 light years thick at the bulge in its center.[16] Many of the distant stars blur together to form the cloudlike clusters we see on a dark clear night and call the Milky Way.

Other galaxies tend to be millions of light years distant, and only two are visible (barely) to the naked eye. We cannot see anything existing in the empty space between the edge of the Milky Way, for instance, and our neighbor galaxy Andromeda. It is hypothesized that enigmatic "dark matter" occupies much of intergalactic space. Perhaps this empty space is also infused with the electromagnetic vibrations of everything else in the Universe.

Each galaxy sends its own unique radio signal into the cosmos, a signal derived from the energy of its every star member. This is a composite signal and not just the random emissions of billions of stars. In some cases these broadcasts emanate not from within the galaxy, but from double lobes located many light years beyond it. Some galaxies are seen to emit more radiation energy into space than can be accounted for by the sum total of their star content. There is no scientific explanation for any of this.

The sky was clear—remarkably clear—
and the twinkling of all the stars seemed to be
but throbs of one body, timed by a common pulse.
—THOMAS HARDY, *FAR FROM THE MADDING CROWD*

Like stars, galaxies come in different sizes with different characteristics. Their shapes also vary. The two commonest shapes are the younger spirals and the older ellipticals. The third basic shape is the irregular—a category that includes any other shape that a galaxy takes. Some of the irregulars may once have been spirals before they were bent out of shape by the gravitational pull of other larger galaxies.

It is predicted that a black hole exists at the heart of most galaxies. Science may never be able to prove the existence of this cosmic magician that is able to suck stars into itself and make them disappear. These improbable entities almost certainly do exist, but it should be pointed out that there is no more hard evidence for black holes than there is for fairies, angels, or astrology. And unlike the latter, there are neither eyewitness reports of black holes, nor do they have much of a history.

The galaxies exert enormous gravitational pulls upon each other, effortlessly, across distances measured in millions of light years. Gravity is what binds Milky Way and Andromeda together with their thirty-odd galactic companions in this particular patch of Universe. We can easily take this invisible force for granted, as it works over vast distances—from one edge of the solar system, or Universe, to the other. And we still know only the laws defining how gravity behaves, having no idea of what it is, or how or why it behaves as it does.

We do understand much about many invisible forces and phenomena such as sound, X-rays, magnetism, radio waves, and the wind. But gravity does not even seem to have an invisible presence—it just is. Or maybe it isn't. Physicists are now unsure of whether gravity even exists, preferring to explain the seeming attraction of objects to each other as due to the curvature of space-time described by Einstein's Theory of Relativity. Meanwhile, they continue to rely upon Newton's understanding of gravity to successfully send rockets to visit other planets.

New forms of telescopes have revealed that galaxies have their own distinct atmospheres, which can be as complex as atmospheres on some of the planets. Clouds of gas move inside and outside of the galaxy, bringing in fresh hydrogen gas from intergalactic space and expelling gas into space on high-speed winds similar in some ways to the solar wind. Galaxies are much more than just an accidental conglomeration of stars; they are entities unto themselves.

Each galaxy is itself bound together by the random velocities and trajectories of all its component stars. We could also say that it is held apart by these trajectories, because if the stars were not all in motion the galaxy would eventually collapse into itself from the gravitational pull of its billions of stars (as did the loose cosmic dust which formed those stars in the first place, according to theory). This random motion of the stars has been compared to that of atoms and molecules moving around within a hot gas. Looking at entire stars moving about as though they were single particles in a hot gas gives us another example of harmonics at vastly different scales.

The Hubble telescope has revealed collisions taking place between galaxies. In these gigantic intergalactic bangs, millions of new stars are created as the cosmic pressures work upon the interstellar dust of the galaxy. In some cases whole populations of stars will be transplanted from one galaxy to another, rotating in different orbits. After one of these collisions, a great halo of stars will sometimes surround the galaxy.

Any one galaxy might contain from tens of millions, to over a trillion stars, and in that part of the Universe visible through telescopes there are over one hundred billion galaxies. These uncountable collections of stars too, are often assembled together into galactic clusters—a grouping of galaxies . . . the mind boggles! Even these clusters of galaxies are grouped into superclusters.

Since the late 20th century, astrophysicists have been studying giant and well-patterned magnetic fields, which connect neighbors in a cluster of galaxies. It is now anticipated that these fields may reach across even greater spans of the cosmos. And it is looking increasingly likely that these magnetic fields stretched across the primordial Universe. Perhaps they played a hand in shaping it.

These little bioelectrical processors in our heads make us feel full of life and purpose. Imagine what it's like to be a giant star, with a magnetic mind-field stretching light years into space. Then assemble billions of these dynamic components into a new entity—a galaxy. What must it be like to have the processing power of billions of stars at your disposal—what do you do with that; what's it like? Though a part of that galaxy, the answer is probably beyond our ever knowing.

Universe
the "all" in "all is one"

. . . He sees and knows that the cosmos, which to the self-conscious
mind seems made up of dead matter, is in fact far otherwise—
is in very truth a living presence. He sees that instead of men
being, as it were, patches of life scattered through an infinite
sea of non-living substance, they are in reality specks
of relative death in an infinite ocean of life.
—R. M. BUCKE, COSMIC CONSCIOUSNESS, 1902

I T WAS LESS than a century ago that we believed our own galaxy to be the sum total of the Universe. We now witness an unending expanse of further galaxies and discover that, like people and stars, these giants of the cosmos get together in groups and clusters. We live in an expanding Universe, one which would not be here, so we are told, if its rate of expansion were to vary by a fraction of a percent.

We once thought the backwards history of the Universe to be infinite, until physicists realized that it had a sudden beginning, calculated to have been 13.7 billion years ago. But ultimately the limits of exploration are reached as we contemplate the totality of the infinite Universe, beyond and before which we can hardly imagine.

We may never be able to fathom the ultimate purpose of this Universe with its uncountable galaxies filled with uncountable stars. But purpose there is—a purpose beyond putting lights in our night sky and helping us to tell the seasons apart, as implied by the Old Testament's Genesis. Over the millennia, many popular religions have implied that the purpose of this Creation was to provide a suitable medium for the development of the human species. Telescopes have shown such a notion to be untenable.

The incredible unlikelihood of this Universe's existence has directly led some physicists to come up with the concept of a Multiverse containing near-infinite numbers of individual universes. With enough universes out there, it is thought conceivable that one of them would have accidentally happened to turn out like this one, with the ever-so-fine parameters needed to support life. This brings to mind the old story about putting infinite monkeys with infinite typewriters to work and discovering that one day, in the course of forever, a monkey unknowingly types out the complete works of William Shakespeare. We know in our bones that those infinite monkeys would never even deliver us Mark Anthony's speech. There are some bizarre theories coming out of physics, underpinned by the absolute faith of physicists in a Universe that is intelligence free—apart from us.

Those who make it their life's work to study the workings of the stars and galaxies would do well to consider the implications of stellar consciousness—remembering that it was a jealous Christian church that originally forbade their consideration of such heretical ideas.

The Universe is a single whole, comprised of many parts that are also wholes.
—**PLATO,** 380 B.C.

It seems apparent that Universe itself is but another level of higher mind—albeit the highest as far as we are concerned. Perhaps each of its countless billions of giant galaxies is the equivalent of a single neuron firing in our own brain. Its invisible mind might be filling the entirety of what we consider to be the empty space between galaxies—a space that is infused with the electromagnetic vibrations of everything else in the Universe. We are assured by modern astrophysicists that the Universe contains *dark energy,* a force they are at a loss to define or explain, but whose existence is essential to their calculations. Could this indefinable "energy" be something to do with universal consciousness—a force unto itself with the ability to hold the cosmos together? Is it a subtle form of electromagnetic energy at work?

Many religions of the East have made the "All is One" point. Giordano Bruno did so in the West, and was consequently burned at the stake by the Church authorities, who clearly held otherwise. The term Pantheism was coined in the 18th century to denote the belief system that is described by the phrase: God is All and All is God. Our individual blood cells may not realize that they are part and parcel of the same organism as our hair, our teeth and the digestive bacteria in our gut. Similarly, that organism—us—is able to function without the knowledge that its own existence is but a microcomponent of a far greater organism that encompasses everything from grains of sand to galaxies, from clouds to comets, from apples to avalanches.

Always think of the universe as one living organism, with a single substance and a single soul; and observe how all things are submitted to the single perceptivity of this one whole, all are moved by its single impulse, and all play their part in the causation of every event that happens. Note the intricacy of the weave, the complexity of the web.
—**MARCUS AURELIUS,** "MEDITATIONS," 121-180 B.C.

The vibration of this Universal Being, its unique code, is manifested as the Chi, Holy Spirit, or Prana—the all-pervasive life force recognized by most religions, presumed to be accessible throughout the Universe. Perhaps it is a vibrational equivalent to the DNA that is present in every cell of our own body (excepting red blood cells), from our hair to our bones, from our fingers to our nerve cells.

Everything—*everything* in this known universe is infused with consciousness. Consciousness is not the basic building block of matter. It is the architect. Why does this Universe exist? What is its destiny? On what does it ponder? And why is it that we humble human beings should find such things to be of interest?

In the light of intelligence
on the intelligence in light

LIGHT IS INVISIBLE, yet it allows us to see. Light hurtles through space for years, yet loses none of its energy in the process. Light can be reduced to a single irreducible particle, the photon, and this photon can be in two places at once. We must wait eight minutes for light to arrive from Sun's surface, but the light itself arrives in no time at all. Light gives substance and form to the vegetable world, yet itself has no physical property or structure. Light is a mystery—and becomes even more so as science discovers ever more of its properties.

A fundamental energy force of the Universe that it saturates, light carries the warmth of the Sun and the vibrations of the stars to Earth. Science is able to harness many of the extraordinary abilities of light and to perform amazing feats with it. Yet physicists can tell us little about the nature of light, nor explain how it is able to do the incredible things that it does. Zoroastrianism, the first great and lasting religion, elevated Ahura Mazda, god of light, to the position of supreme deity. The gOd of Genesis found it necessary to "let there be light" before it was possible to create anything beyond Heaven and a world that had neither form nor substance.

Light is the primary product of Sun to reach our planet; without it there could be no life on Earth. Over a million megatons of pure light energy is released every second from Sun. Can you imagine this? One megaton is the energy released by a million tons of TNT, so this is a million times that—each and every second. Organic life on Earth is designed to receive and utilize this energy. We cannot live on air and water, supplemented by rocks and soil. In a very real sense we, and all other life forms, are built by Sunlight, using our bodies as biological batteries to store and release its solar energy through the process of life.

It is light that provides the essential energy to power photosynthesis, the commonplace daily miracle that takes place in every blade of grass, every plant, shrub and tree on the surface of Earth. Two thirds of the planet's photosynthesis takes place in the oceans, feeding the thousands of phytoplankton living in each drop of water near the ocean's surface. This process takes carbon from CO_2 in the air and, through the energy of light, combines it with hydrogen and oxygen from water to form the carbohydrate building blocks of the vegetable world.

The vegetable products arising from photosynthesis provide the basis of the food chain for all animal life on this planet. Plants take the H out of H_2O and the C out of CO_2, and what's left over is oxygen, which conveniently provides the breath of life for all that animal life. Neat.

Good soil provides a residence and some important nutritional supplements for plants, with DNA supplying the plan, but the basic building blocks of plants are light, air, and water. When we dry and burn plants, the minimal ash that remains represents the small portion that was originally extracted from the soil. The word itself, photosynthesis, means "made by light." Without light there is no life.

The mystery of light has challenged great minds since well before the age of science. Early Greek philosopher-scientists disagreed over whether the light of vision emanated from the eyes, or was received from the outside environment. The arguments of Euclid won the day, based upon Plato's belief that our eyes project the light of our soul outwards, to illuminate objects. This 3rd century B.C. theory prevailed for 1,300 years until the great Arab scientist Al-Hazen described the relationship between reflected light sources, the lens in our eye, and the image we see. His book on optics was translated in the West as Thesaurus Opticus and formed the basis of subsequent European study into light.

In 1678, Christian Huygens proposed the first scientific theory explaining light as a wave-like phenomenon, which explained many of its properties. Shortly afterwards, in 1704, Isaac Newton put forward a rival theory proposing that light was composed of tiny particles, or corpuscles, emitted by luminous bodies. His theory also explained much of light's behavior. Newton had rekindled the science of optics in 1666, after using a prism to divide white light into the rainbow spectrum. As a child I remember being impressed by a simple experiment that involved putting all the colors of the rainbow onto a cardboard disk, looking like a multicoloured pie. When this disk is spun with a simple motor the pie does not turn to mud, but to a clean white, thus demonstrating the colored composition of white light that Newton discovered.

For many years to follow, eminent scientists sought to establish, once and for all, whether light was a wave or a particle phenomenon. Sometimes light seems to travel in waves, like sound moves through the air and waves move through the ocean. Waves do not involve an actual movement of particles—just transference of their energy or organization from one place to another. When a wave travels thousands of meters or miles across the ocean, it is not carrying water molecules with it—that is achieved with currents and flows.

In other circumstances, light behaves like discrete particles—individual things bouncing off other things and relating to them at the same time. Photons of light are particles that move from A to B (as in Sun to Earth) at a constant speed—the speed of light. They start at one physical location and end up at another, unlike water in the ocean's wave, which is transmitting only energy. And when these light particles reach their destination, they react with the particles they hit.

Debate over these theories continued for some 200 years, with further experimentation and discovery producing evidence supporting both camps. Notable among these was the recognition by James Clerk Maxwell in 1864 that visible light is one of the many manifestations of electro-magnetic radiation, constituting but a small slice of the full electromagnetic spectrum, which also includes radio waves, x-rays and many other manifestations of the photon that were once thought to be separate phenomena.

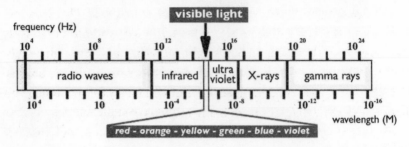

THE ELECTROMAGNETIC SPECTRUM - *different vibrations of the photon*

   Albert Einstein finally resolved the issue in 1905. His special theory of relativity showed that light could travel in waves without the existence of a "luminiferous" ether. This was the hypothetical medium that wave-theory proponents required but had been unable to prove. In the same year he applied Max Planck's quantum theory to show that all forms of electro-magnetic radiation, including light, travel in tiny bundles of energy called photons. The energy of each photon is determined by its frequency. So light was recognized to behave both as a particle and as a wave, depending on which aspect of its behaviour is being explained.

   If all this wave/particle stuff is getting you confused, do not get distressed. At least you will be more able to understand why the greatest minds of science were confused and in controversy over it for such a long time.

   In essence, what we call light is pure elemental energy that is vibrating within the narrow section of the electromagnetic energy spectrum that is visible to the human eye. Electromagnetic energy is counted as one of the four fundamental forces of nature,[17] and visible light is one of its many manifestations. Its force carrier is the photon, which is an elementary irreducible particle—the tiny corpuscular particle of energy that Isaac Newton envisioned 300 years ago. Photons are quite incredible things with amazing abilities. Photons are the electromagnetic energy that enables exchanges to be made between particles. And just what sort of exchanges are we talking about between particles? For a start, if these exchanges were not taking place there would be no way of seeing anything in this world. Photons are, perhaps, the most effective carriers of information we could ever imagine.

Unless we are looking directly at its source, what we call visible light is invisible to us until it first bounces off something else. This is immediately apparent when we look into the night sky and see the planets and moon brightly reflecting Sun's light, which streams through an otherwise dark and invisible space, with only other stars as visible objects. Virtually every point of dark space is saturated with electromagnetic radiation including the light from many millions of stars and galaxies.

We take for granted our ability to see things around us but vision is by no means easy to explain. The things that we look at do not project an image of themselves into the air. It is the light—countless quadrillions of photons—which has first taken a look at them, and then conveyed the relevant information about them to all around. When we see the color red, the scientific explanation is that the red object has absorbed all the other colors of the spectrum comprising white light, and only reflected the red back into space. To put it more simply, the photons have left something with the object, and now carry away information about that object with them.

We mainly view the result of light and matter's electromagnetic exchange as being the determinant of whether things are one color or another. Perhaps, however, there is more going on in this electromagnetic exchange, and the varying colors we perceive are but the by-product of a more fundamental process taking place. After all, photons of light make exchanges with literally every particle of matter that they touch, through an interaction with its electrons. Perhaps light is picking up other information, along with the color of matter that it touches?

We do not know whether the electrons on the surface of objects with which light collides are equipped to read any information from the light about their own surroundings, visible or otherwise. Take plants, for example. We now understand that plants breathe in air and expel it through a process known as transpiration, even though they have no lungs, as we know them. They absorb water and nutrients from the soil, taken up through their roots, and this is pumped through veins to all parts of the organism. They do this without a stomach or a heart, as we know them. Many gardeners swear by the ability of plants to respond to their spoken encouragement and to music, even though they have no ears, as we

know them. Might plants also be able to perceive aspects of their surroundings, even though they do not possess eyes, as we know them?

The means to receive information about the local environment,
through an eye-like organ, is a facility that is common to virtually all
animal life forms, with few exceptions. Plants are far more tuned into
the light than are we animals, relying on light-sensitive specialized cells
to absorb the life-energy of photons, thus powering the photosynthesis
that gives them form. Perhaps plants possess a means to read some of
the information these photons are carrying, and we simply do not possess the means to recognize this faculty.

Astrophysicists are able to analyse the photons arriving from a distant star and determine how far away it is, how big it is, its chemical
composition, its age and describe its unique electromagnetic signature.
Whether transmitted in waves or indivisible packets, light energy carries a considerable amount of information with it. Although the light
from a distant star may have sped through space for hundreds of years,
travelling 300,000 kilometers in every second of the journey, the individual photons have neither faded nor lost any of their energy when they
finally arrive at the back of our eyeball, or on the lens of a telescope. The
variable photon is a hardy item indeed, and distinct enough that just one
of them can be detected by the eyeball of a frog in the dark.

Consider how efficiently light does carry information. More than 99
percent of Sun's photons will just travel forever, carrying their signal
undiminished across the infinity of space, encountering little other than
other photons on their journey. Just a miniscule proportion of the tiny
proportion that reaches Earth might strike a persons face 100 meters
away from you, and at that point will bounce off in all directions. Just
a fraction of a percent of this "bounce" will reach your eyes and bring
with it enough information for you to recognize the person and maybe
even read their emotions. Collect a few more photons with a telescope
lens and you could see the mole on their chin, or recognize them from
kilometers away. How can anything be so efficient?

Even though an irreducible photon has no sub-components, it is able
to carry an astounding variety of information. While we assume (rightly
or wrongly) that all electrons, protons, quarks, and other elementary

particles are identical to each other, there is no question that photons are not. It does indeed seem as though any individual photon has the capacity to assume a unique state that has never before been achieved by any photon in the history of the Universe. Unlike snowflakes, they are not all distinct from one another, but each has the capacity to be unique—to carry specific information that has never before existed.

Light can be gentle, dangerous, dreamlike, bare, living, dead, misty, clear, hot, dark, violet, spring-like, falling, straight, sensual, limited, poisonous, calm and soft.
—SVEN NYKVIST, SWEDISH CINEMATOGRAPHER

In 1982, a team at the Institute of Optics in Paris, led by Alain Aspect, was able to demonstrate a form of communication between photons. In their experiment, they produced two "twinned" photons and sent them off in opposite directions at the speed of light. Thereafter, they were seen to instantly co-ordinate their polarizations, demonstrating a form of communication that exceeded the speed of light (like thought?). They are said to be "entangled," and any action on one of them will affect the other—even though they may be light years apart. Physicists are understandably still puzzled over how this is done, and mathematicians are at pains to find a way to describe the process. It has now been demonstrated that electrons, and probably atoms, can become entangled, and there is no theoretical limit to the number of entanglements that a photon can make. Sunlight that showers upon us might still be entangled with particles of the star in which it was born.

For a photon there is no time and it is, essentially, everywhere on its own trajectory at once. This appears strange to us. Science fiction often trades on Einstein's Theory of Relativity, conjuring it out of the possibility that if we could travel faster than the speed of light then the clock would reverse for us—taking us backwards in time. Not being able to do this, we exist in a universe where our own arrow of time travels in one direction only—forward. However, for anything traveling at the speed of light, time would not move, or even exist. Thus, because the photon travels at the speed of light, its own journey is instantaneous. Although you and I will age eight minutes while a photon travels from Sun to Earth—as far as the photon is concerned, it arrives at the same time it left.

Although scientists cannot explain how light does what it does, they continue to find more and more applications for its dazzling abilities. The discovery of the laser in 1958 is still yielding new technological uses. Today, photons are rapidly replacing electrons as the most efficient means to manage and transmit information. Moving more electrons requires more wire to move them in, whereas light can just be compressed into optic cable without limit, since it is not matter. The science of optics has made huge strides in the 300 years since Isaac Newton played around with a prism and split white light into its components. And discovery continues in this field, a rare area of science that still shows more potential for mystery and wonder than for comprehension and explanation.

Now that we have covered this much on light, let us consider one more thing about Sunlight. Whether its source is the Sun or a flashlight, light radiates in all directions. We do not express any wonder at the fact that using a flashlight at night enables us to see everything illuminated by its beam. The light is bouncing back with the information, carrying it on a two-way street through the bright white outgoing beams of the flashlight. The flashlight does not dazzle its own information backflow, as it does our eyes when we look directly at its beam. Undoubtedly, the light that Sun showers on our planet is also bouncing back to Sun with a clear and highly detailed picture of Earth, if anybody's watching.

Perhaps Sun is also a giant eye in the sky, reading the returning photons by some means. Perhaps those fine red spicules in its chromosphere have something to do with it. Our vision gets all its information from the light coming through the pupil, that small black circle in the middle of the eye. By capturing more photons through the bigger circle of a telescope lens we see the moons of distant planets and mountain ranges on

Mars. If Sun does have a faculty of sight then it's not going to be through a little lens like our eye, or even through something as awesome as the Hubble telescope, which can spot stars being born in distant galaxies.

We can only guess that if the Sun could see, then its lens would probably be the size of . . . the Sun. The resolution would be some hundreds of billions of times higher than Hubble. The Sun could have an absolutely wonderful view of its planets and of other stars and distant galaxies. It is receiving light from all directions at all times and its lens is simply gargantuan. Together with the "visual" information coming into Sun are the electromagnetic signals sent out by its neighbors in this galaxy, and the unified signals sent out by other distant galaxies.

Regardless of the mechanics, physics and optics that might explain how our local star could be operating with the facility of sight, it appears reasonable that by some means the very source and creator of light itself—that which illuminates our world—is itself equipped to see what is going on in its solar system. This isn't exactly a novel concept either—Sun as an all-seeing gOd. It was central to many of the world's largest cultures of the pre-Christian era, and led to some of the most lasting monuments of earlier civilizations.

Here is a quote from the Encyclopedia Britannica on the general subject of solar-based religions (some religions just had Sun as one of the gods): "Sun is the bestower of light and life to the totality of the cosmos; *with his unblinking, all-seeing eye;* he is the stern guarantor of justice; with the almost universal connection of light with enlightenment or illumination; Sun is the source of wisdom."

As it happens, the single gOd of Judaism, Christianity and Islam is also perceived to be an all-seeing type of character—a divine being who is always watching over us. As they put it in Psalm 94 verse 9: "He that planted the ear, shall he not hear? He that formed the eye, shall he not see?" We know that light is a carrier of energy and information without equal. Does it not seem credible that the local originator of this energy has a use for it, as well as making it a gift of sustenance to the solar system and all the energy systems within it?

When we consider that light does not experience time, enabling it to be everywhere at once, then it helps us to understand the reports brought back by unexpected returnees from the realms of light beings. Frequent accounts from those having near-death experiences tell of leaving their bodies and witnessing their entire lives flashing by *in an instant*, and in full detail, while in spirit form. Though the life review may be ordered chronologically, the experience of it would be outside of time—in the existence of a being of light.

As far as we can discern, the sole purpose of human existence is to kindle a light in the darkness of mere being.
—CARL JUNG

But what of light itself, this great and ongoing mystery? Consider for a moment the ways in which we use light in our own language. When an important concept or situation is understood by us, we "see the light," often because someone else has been "shedding light" on the subject. "Enlightenment" is the term given to the peak of spiritual experience— the state of total understanding and bliss. We revere the "divine light" of the Lord and when somebody is inspired, we speak of the "light in his or her eyes." When we find true love, we have met the "light of our life." We use terms like, "in light of what you have said" or "in the light of experience." When we leave this body, the "lights go out," and when we're very much alive we are "lit up" or "all fired up." We want to be "illuminated" on things from time to time, and don't we always enjoy being "de*light*ed"? Intelligent people will be called "bright" and great ideas and thoughts are called "brilliant." Especially impressive ideas or beauty can be termed "dazzling."

Although not a linguist, I would bet that most languages of the world use similar light-related words to describe concepts associated with intelligence, understanding, and spirituality. It seems to be innate. The root of the word "divine" stems from the Indo-Germanic "div," meaning to shine or give light.

Don't you wish there were a knob on the TV
to turn up the intelligence? There's one marked
"Brightness," but it doesn't work.
—GALLAGHER

As difficult as it may be for our brains to comprehend, our linguistic "body language" intuitively connects light with the intelligent aspect of life. Could it be that light itself is intelligence and that the irreducible photon is the smallest "particle" of intelligence in the Universe? Unlike the atom, we will not be finding ever smaller "sub-photonic" particles—of this we can be sure. Yet this irreducible photon is infinitely variable and capable of receiving and transmitting all manner of information from place to place—at high speed.

Thought is great and swift and free,
the light of the world,
and the chief glory of man.
—BERTRAND RUSSELL

If our "body language" is correct, and light itself is a manifestation of intelligence then it is not inconceivable that it could organize into some form of entity. The intelligence of individual photons may be miniscule, but their ability to compress without forcible constraint is unique. Virtually every spiritual tradition on the planet refers to radiant beings of light—intelligent entities that exist on a parallel plane to our own. We will find very few references to beings of water, air, clay, rock, or any substance other than light in this context. Perhaps intelligence could not exist without the energy of light, the energy that powers existence.

Photons are described as unique in possessing energy and momentum, with no mass. They are a manifestation of energy and information that is without any physical property or substance. Does this not also describe our own thoughts—that which goes on in our minds? Ideas have no mass, although they possess both energy and information. We do not increase in weight when deep in thought. Might the energy of our mind itself be some close electromagnetic cousin of the photon—some harnessing of light energy? Might the very Chi or Prana of our Universe be a primal manifestation of electromagnetic energy, in a vibration not yet detectable by our existing technology?

Perhaps light, the major component of the electromagnetic force saturating our Universe, is itself the Universal Mind, and the Universe we know is but its physical body and organ of re-generation. The photon energy of this force is the E component of Albert Einstein's famous equation $E = mc^2$. Was all this once energy, and is energy that to which it all returns?

From within or from behind, a light shines through us upon things, and makes us aware that we are nothing, but the light is all.

—RALPH WALDO EMERSON

Chaos, the invisible architect
controlling it is not the way to order

THOUGH QUANTUM THEORY is over a century old, we are still grappling with the impact of its discoveries about the behavior and nature of matter. Chaos theory, a relative youngster born in the late 1970s, is no easier to grasp, dealing with realizations about the organized behavior of systems that have no organizer. When enough different elements, or factors in a system, are interacting with each other, and there is no way to determine or definitely predict just what any one part will do, the system is termed "chaotic" by scientists. Another appropriate word to use would be "free."

You need chaos in your soul to give birth to a dancing star.
—NIETZSCHE

The startling discovery of chaos theory is the frequency with which order and harmony spontaneously arise in such chaotic systems, and how sensitive the whole system is to the slightest changes within it. Chaos theory has given rise to many new fields of science, described by names such as complexity theory, nonlinear dynamics, anti-chaos theory, dynamical systems theory, and so on.

Chaos theory is a science that provides strong circumstantial evidence, though of course no proof, for manifestations of intelligence radically different to our own. But non-brain-based intelligence is so outside the scientific status quo that it is seldom, if ever, acknowledged by those who study chaos theory. The "chaos" in chaos theory shares its meaning with ancient cultures. Before Babylon rose to prominence in the ancient world, Chaos was perceived as the mysterious space between Heaven and Earth, and the source of inspiration, form and change in this world. This ancient perception of chaos turns out to be closer to today's scientific interpretation than it is to that we find in news headlines cataloguing the latest disorders of the day.

Chaos theory studies how rainforests or weather systems achieve stability and balance without anybody centrally programming or co-ordinating the multiple components of each system. Chaos theory has enabled the existing sciences—from geology and biology to physics—to look at the wholeness of their subject. Chaos theory recognizes that the synchronicity that so often astounds us in life is a manifestation of the patterned web that connects our universe together. And there is not any one theory to it—any more than there is one theory to biology or physics.

We adore chaos because we love to produce order.
—M.C. **ESCHER**

It was around 2000 B.C. that human culture began to shift away from acknowledging and respecting the positive and creative powers of Chaos, moving instead towards fearing its unpredictability and seeking to control and direct it.[18] This paradigm shift is classically depicted by the Babylonian myth in which Marduk, the symbol of man's control, kills Tiamet, the dragon goddess of Chaos. In many traditional cultures, including those of the Chinese and Celts, the dragon represents the organized but uncontrollable forces of nature. In most Far Eastern cultures the dragon is still respected, and they certainly have no tradition of revering dragon-killers.

The cherished symbol of St. George killing the dragon appears to represent the modern Western affirmation that man can vanquish the chaos and force the world to do his bidding. As the atmosphere heats up and the icecaps melt; as tsunamis shatter coastlines and new epidemics threaten our species; as some turn themselves into bombs while others stockpile bombs designed to flatten cities; as financial institutions collapse and stock markets crash, it seems apparent that the anticipated level of control has not been achieved.

We have injured the dragon in our contrived and concerted efforts to force nature into submission, all the while pumping her full of our toxic wastes. Increasingly in our own society, the dragon energy of chaos and spontaneity is being regulated out of existence. Increasingly we witness, and suffer personally, from the consequences of St. George's approach to providing world order, whether that's needing a license to sing or dance in most public places, being filmed and fined by machines, or living in fear of terrorists and police oppression.

When man interferes with the Tao,
the sky becomes filthy,
the earth becomes depleted,
the equilibrium crumbles,
creatures become extinct.

LAO TSU, *TAO TE CHING*, TRANSLATION BY DR WAYNE DYER

The capacity of the world to create harmony on its own—to create a pattern within a multitude of events—is one that has been glimpsed by mystics, artists and assorted individuals throughout history. By the late 1970s, a handful of scientists and mathematicians were starting to examine this natural order, playing around with new ideas and strange experiments. One of the experiments involved devoting a computer to running a simulated weather system for months on end; another hooked up a few hundred dollars worth of equipment to the dripping tap of a kitchen sink in Santa Cruz, California.

An accident on the computerized weather system revealed that the tiniest change to a large complex system would sooner or later affect the condition of the entire system. This is the so-called Butterfly Effect, discovered and named by Edward Lorenz. He later said that he wished he'd named it after the seagull, a bird with a bigger wing flap, and therefore a more credible influence upon a hurricane 9 months later! For those who are not familiar with this principle it demonstrates how changing a moment in the wind speed of a weather system, by the equivalent of a passing butterfly's wing flap (or seagull if you like), could make the difference between rain and hurricane a year later and thousands of miles away.

If the Butterfly Effect seems somewhat far-fetched to you, then consider an equivalent triviality in your own life. Something as simple as pausing to pass wind, look at an ad, smell a flower, or check the time, could lead to missing a bus, whereby you meet somebody at the bus stop. The plot could go anywhere from here but that meeting could lead to a new occupation, a life-long relationship or just trigger you to read a book that will alter, as does everything in life, the direction of your life thereafter.

The technical term for the Butterfly Effect is "sensitive dependence on initial conditions." Is not every moment an initial condition of the unfolding future? The lesson of this is that every single thing that happens on Earth is a working part of the system of this planet. And, to put it bluntly, that it is worth considering our individual actions because they do count.

The dripping tap in Santa Cruz demonstrated a capacity for self-organization in a relatively simple complex system, which would appear or disappear with the slightest change to the flow rate. The time gaps between dripping drops would actually settle into a pattern, and Robert Shaw, who initiated the experiment, devised a means to visually represent the pattern, which was itself an important contribution to the science. As well as studying dripping taps, chaos theorists recognized the consistent and orderly ways that things such as coastlines, mountain ranges, and banks of clouds are able to develop and structure themselves.

Chaos theory has overturned three centuries of absolute scientific belief in determinism—the idea that with enough data and computing, science could predict the outcome of just about anything. It found that even if you crammed an infinite number of chips into an infinite number of computers and monitored every point and parameter on Earth, you still would not be able to predict, with 100 percent accuracy, the weather at 4 p.m. tomorrow, let alone at 4 p.m. in 3 months' time. Could it be making its mind up as it goes?

Chaos theory has also helped balance the scientific trend towards ever more reductionism, providing a means to look at the activities and patterns of whole systems, rather than just examining their parts, and parts of parts, and parts of parts of parts and so forth. The fractal geometry developed by Benoit Mandelbrot provides the mathematical tools that are needed to describe and examine the real world, where freedom (or scientifically speaking, chaos) reigns. It is a world full of natural order, whether in the structure of a mountain range, the branching of trees, assemblies of clouds or the fractal structure of our lungs which, with every breath we take, exposes a surface area the size of a tennis court to the atmosphere.

Before Mandelbrot, there was no way for scientists to mathematically describe the structure of trees, mountains, clouds, circulatory systems, and many other natural forms based upon self-similarity. Such items could only be drawn, described, or have their measurements taken. In some of the Earth sciences, it must have been like being a meteorologist when tools were first invented that could measure air pressure and humidity.

The more that we develop tools and techniques to study the natural world, the more we find a natural order, a weaving together of everything into an intricately integrated system. This interwoven world has long appeared to be cleverly constructed, and now science is proving this to be so—describing its order and harmony in numbers. Science is able to work with the natural order to a greater degree than was ever possible before.

As yet there has been little investigation into any source for the architecture behind these recognizable and definable, yet inexplicable occurrences of order and harmony. Perhaps the simple reason for this is the sheer inconceivability to so many that any form of intelligence or consciousness could exist that is not both created and contained by a physical brain, preferably one of ours.

Inanimate Intelligence
might stuff be smarter than we think?

FROM TIME immemorial, owners of crystals who tune into their vibrational energy have claimed to experience what feels like a transmission and receipt of intelligent energies between themselves and the crystal. Have these people been deceived by crystals for all these years? Would my enriching and uplifting experiences with the lovely amethyst crystal upon my desk have been equally attainable if I had believed as strongly in the powers of a crumpled tin can or a potato? I doubt it, although science would have us believe as much, until such time, of course, as it is able to explain the phenomena that make a difference. Crystals are, after all, inanimate and supposed to be devoid of any potential for a causal relationship with human beings.

But first of all, where do we draw the line between that which is animate and that which is inanimate? There are quite different opinions as to where this important divide lies, although nobody seems to be arguing very much about it. Animate is derived from the Latin *animare*, meaning to make alive, which comes from *anima*, meaning breath or spirit.

Most scientists will still draw a distinct divide between the animal world and everything else. They regard humans, ants and amoeba as animate; trees, algae, rocks and rivers as inanimate. But common usage of the term "inanimate" is shifting that boundary. When comparing ten dictionary definitions for "inanimate," in print and on the Internet, I found that contrary to scientific usage, only two of them clearly treated plants as inanimate. The other eight, represented by the three below, either specifically excluded plants from inanimate, or left it open for us to decide.

Inanimate definitions

Cambridge Dictionary of American English: *possessing none of the characteristics of life that an animal or plant has.*

Dictionary.com: *Not having the qualities associated with active, living organisms.*

Webster Dictionary, 1913: *Not animate; destitute of life or spirit; lifeless; dead; inactive; dull; as, stones and earth are inanimate substances.*

The great divide surely lies between living breathing things with clear beginnings, transitions, and ends—and all the other elements of the non-breathing inanimate world with which they share existence.

Plants are without question living organisms and active ones, though their activity is of a different order to animal activity. Perhaps science has just neglected to reclassify plants after recognizing that they too breathe, through the process of transpiration. Plants move as they spread roots deep into the earth to seek foundation and nourishment, while breaking through concrete if necessary, to reach the light above. Their flowers open and close, they have sex with each other (lots of it given the opportunity), and disperse their seeds.

Plants develop elaborate defences against predators, and form extraordinary alliances with other plants and animals. The techniques used to protect and propagate their seeds may involve anything from being carried off by the breeze, getting eaten and expelled by an animal, or coming to life through the agency of a destructive fire. Plants even share human characteristics that we recognize (cells, sex, territorial tendencies) and share much of their genetic coding with us, half or more in some cases, as with bananas and cabbage. They share our ancestry, after all, in the family of life.

The more that science discovers about the inner workings and strategies of the vegetable world the more and more probable it seems that intelligence does pervade the entire living world, from mankind to microbe, from tree to fungi. But what about the inanimate world of rocks and mountains, grains of sand and crystals, winds and hurricanes, blazing stars and galaxies? What about plastic chairs and paperclips—is there intelligence here?

Intelligence is most commonly defined as the ability to absorb and understand information, and to use that understanding. Intelligence enables its receptacles to learn and adapt and respond. In Webster's 1913 edition it is elegantly described as *"The act or state of knowing; the exercise of the understanding."* I will use this definition when looking at inanimate stuff.

Before we get carried away though, let us recognize that I am extending the horizons of intelligence, lowering the bar on how much "understanding" is being exercised, if you like. We could take the academic approach and determine three or thirteen defined categories of intelligence from the elemental to the cosmic with ours located somewhere in between. But even then, we are sometimes capable of straying outside our "norm," plunging into base elemental regions or soaring into the cosmic.

From the traditional viewpoint of the animist, a universal consciousness permeates every particle of matter in the Universe, from the electrons in your socks to the thundercloud about to soak them. If these particles of matter do possess some awareness of being, some miniscule micro-bit of consciousness, it becomes less surprising that they are able to self-organize into something with form and order, something with behavior that seems intelligent. This "something" might be a whole weather system or a single thundercloud, an ocean or a rolling river, a mountain range or an ordered beach, a star or a volcano.

Mountaineers and seafarers have long attributed character and personality to the realms they explore, as did the early astronomers, before the thought of it was banned. Without allowing for anything other than brain-based intelligence, we must view all this stuff as chemical and physical reactions, accidentally bringing about complex functioning phenomena, some of which are even able to support intelligent life.

A giant ocean full of intelligence might be dependent upon that which exists within its every drop. If we can accept James Lovelock's Gaia hypothesis of a global planetary system operating as though there is intelligence at play, then we can logically accept that the sub-components of this system form an integral part of that intelligence. We recognize a similar concept in the group intelligence of a termite mound or a slime mould, seeing it as a composite of its individual components. Perhaps intelligence will always be a by-product of consciousness—perhaps even it is the purpose of consciousness.

The weather systems of the world and its great oceans bear many hallmarks of intelligence, and have an enormous impact upon the planet. Individual weather systems and oceans have characters and cycles unique to themselves, manifesting all manner of coherent activity and organization. Oceans develop major currents and flows, running on and below the surface as they shift masses of water around the planet. Oceans moisten the planet's atmosphere and provide a home to the enormous algae blooms that help maintain the gaseous-balance of the air we breathe. Oceans are home to most of the life on planet Earth.

Life is the fire that burns and the sun that gives light.
Life is the wind and the rain and the thunder in the sky.
Life is matter and is earth, what is and what is not,
and what beyond is in Eternity.
—THE UPANISHADS, TRANSLATION BY THOMAS WYATT

The weather systems of the world are constantly receiving information and responding to it, as currents of air transverse the globe and communities of clouds assemble to drift across it. Of course, we have some understanding of how the factors of wind speed, pressure, humidity and temperature combine to create clouds and complex weather systems. But our understanding of the mechanics of a thundercloud does not, not for a moment, deny the existence of a nebulous intelligence within it—any more than understanding our DNA and how blood cells oxygenate denies our own intelligence.

Through an electron microscope we can see the highly patterned molecular structure of crystals, though we have no idea how that organization is achieved. Although the incredible ability of crystals to manage information is utilized in the microchips of all the world's computers, we seldom question what part its incredible molecular organization might play in the program of a living planet. Whilst the cultivation of crystals destined for computer chips can be accelerated so that they grow to size in weeks, rather than thousands of years, the starting point can only be natural seed crystal, supplied by planet Earth. In the early days of radio, the ability of crystals to "read" airborne electromagnetic vibrations enabled enthusiasts to build their own cheap radios with nothing more than a piece of crystal, some wire, and a sensitive headphone. No electrical input was required.

Might it be that crystals are purposefully self-designed to receive electromagnetic waves, and to store and transmit information of some sort? Perhaps they know something of what is going on, and it is not so silly to believe in the transfer of energies with crystals. Perhaps the standard sci-fi movie use of crystals as receivers and transmitters of information draws on our own deep intuitive knowledge, and not just their potential for stunning light effects. We can but wonder at what goes on within the highly organized atomic structure of a crystal. The primary component of the 40 kilometer deep crust of Earth is silica, in quartz as silicon dioxide. Perhaps this is a functional phenomenon.

I am not suggesting that something need be as organized as a crystal or as complex as an ocean to display intelligence, but they are clearly better examples than rocks or plastic chairs. The capacity for intelligence in any physical phenomenon is likely to be related closely to its ability to create or utilize energy. Thus when the energy finally leaves our body, so too does data and intelligence as our vehicle returns to raw ingredients.

When the hurricane hits land and dissipates, so too does it return to original components. Even stars go out, eventually.

Added to this energy potential would be the four factors of complexity, age, size, and experience. Thus oceans would have more capacity for intelligence than ponds; crystals more than rocks; cars more than penknives; humans more than mice; stars more than planets and a hurricane more than a whirlwind in the supermarket car park. A much-played saxophone has more spirit than its brother collecting dust in the attic. Even the humble plastic chair may have some scope for intelligence, though perhaps it is the relative "stupidity" of plastic—its very inability to react with most other elements—that makes it of such value to us.

Entertaining, for a moment, the idea that there may be a basic capacity for consciousness and intelligence in rocks, scissors and passing clouds, albeit quite different from that in worms, trees and human beings—how could this intelligence be operating?

THE ELECTRON CONNECTION

Perhaps electrons hold the key—perhaps they *are* the key. Everything that manifests as matter in this world contains atoms surrounded by orbiting electrons. What are electrons? That's a tough question since it is difficult, bordering on impossible, to examine an electron. One of the underlying premises of quantum physics maintains that electrons are indistinguishable from one another. This may be true from the point of view of our ability to distinguish, but does not require that they are all identical. We know that electrons get excited and emit electrons. Is it unreasonable to suggest that an excited electron differs from an unexcited one, whether we can notice the difference or not?

A startling insight into the world of electrons arose during experiments carried out in 1942 at the Berkeley Radiation Laboratory in Berkeley, California. Quantum physicist David Bohm created a soup-like plasma containing free electrons and positive ions (positively charged atoms). To his surprise, the electrons started to organize their activities and perform coordinated tasks, as though they were part of a larger whole. As F. David Peat put it: "As he studied the plasmas he became struck by their extraordinary nature. They began to take on, for him, the qualities of living beings."[19] It was difficult for Bohm to avoid the conclusion that each individual electron is equipped to receive and process information about its surrounding environment.

Another larger plasma soup of electrons that is 4.8 million kilometers wide orbits Jupiter within its magnetic field. If anybody knew what to look for, they would probably notice this electric soup entity putting its organizing abilities to good use, making its own contribution to the balance of the solar system.

The almost weightless subatomic electron is a curious mixture of part matter and part concept. It exists and is a recognizable phenomenon with specific properties, but it is hard to define or pin down as an object or particle. Quantum physics will confuse even more with an explanation of the "Copenhagen interpretation." This concludes that electrons only manifest as a physical object when an observer is looking at them. At that moment, none of the electron's other properties are discernible. It must be frustrating trying to study them. As electrons jump from one ring to another of the atom they orbit, they do so without travelling the distance between. We'd call this teleportation—physicists call it the quantum leap.

It seems as though electrons could be photons trapped within a physical body—a form of light that is bound to the material "flesh" of the atom. Electrons certainly seem to be close relatives of photons, sharing various unusual features including the ability to communicate instantaneously with each other. These quantum particles also appear to get on with each other. Whenever light-bearing photons strike an object, a small exchange with the electrons in that object is logged by quantum physics as the photons bounce back, now carrying information from that object.

Light itself, whether produced by Sun, a matchstick, light bulbs, or deep-sea fish is always the product of excited electrons releasing a photon. This happens as they make their leap from one orbit of their atom's nucleus to another, or when they are affected by a magnetic field, such as the corona of a star. Quantum physicists have created situations where an electron meets a short-lived positron (an electron with a positive charge) and they turn into two light photons. The phenomenon has been described as a kind of "shape-shifting."

In the chapter on light, I proposed that light itself is the raw material of intelligence. Considering their familiarity with photons leads me to suggest that any intelligence at play in matter is likely to be channelled and managed by the electrons within it. Electrons have been seen to demonstrate entanglement in the same way as photons—remembering the meeting of another electron and coordinating aspects of their behavior thereafter. The electrons in David Bohm's plasma soup organized and coordinated their activities. We have to ask: Might electrons retain a small remnant of their coordinating skills when they are a component of "solid" matter as well as when they are part of a charged plasma in a quantum physics laboratory experiment? Perhaps it is those skills that enable matter to display the remarkable characteristics that make it what it is.

We once assumed that the properties of matter arise solely from the physical structure of the atoms and molecules comprising it, somehow working like simple building bricks that make big solid things from small solid things. But this assumption was a simple act of faith, though more rational, perhaps, than belief in the virgin birth. The more that quantum physics delves into the innermost workings of the physical material world, the more difficult it becomes to comprehend how matter works. A question as simple as "Why is wood solid?" can assume the status of a fundamental mystery for which there is no rational explanation.

Matter does not seem nearly as solid as it appears, once the role of the electron is taken into consideration. We have all been taught about the atom, with its nucleus of protons and neutrons, surrounded by rings of orbiting electrons. Infinitesimal electrons define the boundary of a carbon atom, whether it is manifesting as charcoal or diamond. Let us imagine the nucleus of an atom of carbon to be a small orange, and six sesame seeds to be the electrons orbiting it. Scaled to size, how far away from the nucleus of the atom would we find our border-defining electrons? In the quantum world there is no exact answer to this, but the distance from our orange to the sesame seeds would be measured in kilometers, not centimeters. Most of matter, it now seems, is comprised of "empty" space.

There is no hard outer edge to an atom—it is described as being more like a fuzzy cloud of orbiting electrons. Much of what takes place within the subatomic world of quantum particles is beyond any logic or explanation—though the understanding of its mechanics enables our highest technology to work. Quantum physicists are fond of pointing out that anybody who professes to understand what is going on in quantum physics has not studied the field sufficiently. They are right about that.

The nucleus of a carbon atom is the same whether it manifests as smoke, charcoal, graphite or diamond. It is the electrons that bind them together differently. Combined with oxygen, carbon becomes CO_2—a clear gas and the breath of life for plants. Add the carbon from CO_2 to water and light to bring substance to plants. When harmless hydrogen is combined with poisonous chlorine gas, we get hydrochloric acid. Combine poisonous chlorine with volatile sodium and we get harmless table salt.[20]

When matter is involved in chemical combinations and reactions such as the above, natural and man-made, it is *only* the electrons that are making the changes, determining which other atoms to combine with, and what the end product or products are going to look like, feel like or do. The atom's heavy nucleus of protons and neutrons remains undisturbed in chemical reactions, being altered only in a nuclear reaction.

Whether they are all identical or not, perhaps matter's electrons, like light, have some capacity to carry information or even intelligence. Do they know somehow what they are and how they behave?

KNOWING MATTER

Though my postulations above about intelligence in electrons may be a flight of fancy, our ability to correctly explain phenomena will have no effect upon the mechanics of any particular phenomenon. There is a level of coherence existing, from that of the entire cosmos to that existing within a single bacterium that seems beyond the possibility of accident and coincidence. Although it might appear simplistic, it is not unreasonable to suggest that the reason things "hang together" so well is because every thing contains some measure of intelligence, together with an awareness of being, belonging and form. Until they are willing to include intelligence in their considerations, scientists may never be able to explain how natural phenomena from slime molds to weather systems to stars manage to achieve and maintain their incredible feats of self-organization.

This next observation even seems a little silly to me, and cosmic it certainly is not, but from the age of 19 I have been buying paperclips in boxes, and in all the intervening years I have never ceased to be impressed by their propensity to link together into chains of ridiculous length. I once counted nine in a link, and wonder what the world record on these chaotic linkages would be. But it was not until working on this book that I experimented with casually brushing two paperclips together at different angles to see how easy it is to join them without intent, pressure or force. Try it yourself. We use string, rope and wires to tie and bind and connect things together. Perhaps we should not be surprised by how readily our earphone leads or any string-like things get hopelessly intertwined while resting undisturbed in a drawer. Could these fabrications of ours know that they are designed for joining and binding things together and behave accordingly? It sometimes seems like it.

Can matter itself transfer information in a method and format that we could scarcely imagine, of a nature that we cannot measure? Though neither tree nor rock nor winding river is able to comprehend a newspaper, they may be equipped to comprehend forms of data that we cannot. The mountain range, the weather system, and the ocean may have means to be aware of their existence and role in the local and larger environment. Perhaps to some degree they also manage and enjoy their own existence. For thousands of years, to the primitive untrained human mind, it did seem obvious that these complex phenomena were conscious players in the world.

The experience of intelligence would be vastly different for different forms. It is difficult for us to empathize with a big rock or the river rushing around it, and any intelligence they possess would not involve free will as we enjoy it. Though intelligence would not give a rock the ability to "do" anything in the way that we understand doing, it might still give it an ability to subtly interact with the surrounding environment. Perhaps this rock could store information or "memories" of some sort, and subtly influence events around it.

Human beings have long acknowledged the powers of matter through our veneration of inanimate objects or places, which are thought to contain a special vibration or power. This quality could be inherent, such as that in a large clear crystal, an enchanted spring, or a standing stone. Power can be invested though the arrangement of items, such as the stones of Stonehenge, a cathedral's altar or a pentacle drawn upon the ground. Great historical events, or even sporting events, can invest power in the battle standard of a regiment or the football that scored a trophy-winning point.

Mystical powers are accorded to anything associated with an ancient seer, saint, or prophet—whether it be bones, a shroud, clothes, jewelry, hair, dried blood, or even footprints. Venerated relics play an important part in most religious and cultural traditions. Throughout their existence, the finger-bones of a saint were immersed in his or her vibrations—the electrons within it in constant entanglement with the electromagnetic aura of that person. During centuries of careful preservation and constant veneration, these bones may have intermingled with the charged auras of millions more, adding power to them in the process. Great importance is accorded these items, though some might assert they have no more relevance than the knucklebones of a slaughtered pig.

Collectors pay large sums of money to own something related to important people, be they famous statesmen or rock stars. Although this can be investment driven, there is a core value ascribed to possessing some faint vibration of John Lennon, Marilyn Monroe, Winston Churchill, or Albert Einstein. After all, some of the electrons in that auctioned stocking once entangled with the electrons in Marilyn's legs, and those in the hat with the mind of Einstein.

Practitioners of feng shui recognize the importance of situating objects in harmony with their surrounding environment. They believe that objects and buildings are "happier" when they are in the right location—and that it is better for us to live in a happy building than an unhappy one. It would be rare for any major building to be constructed in the Far East without the enlistment of a feng shui expert on the project.

Most top chefs will treat their knives with great respect, beyond that needed just to keep them sharp and hygienic. They have a relationship with their knives. Many musicians will feel the same way about their instruments, after sharing so many magic moments with them. And "Betsy," my friend Michael Bell's yellow '52 Buick convertible, has decidedly added a real personality to its machine intelligence after many years on the road—and Mike's loving attention.

Never fight an inanimate object.
—P.J. O'ROURKE

Whenever we channel prayers or requests to specially revered objects or sites, we demonstrate our belief in the ability of inanimate objects and phenomena to have an effect upon our lives. I have suggested before that we might regularly be exposed to the minor influence of inanimate objects in our daily lives. All that might be required of them is the slightest tweak to the subtle field of our thought process. How often have you lost things that later seem to "find you," rather than you finding them? Or happened to glance in the right direction at just the right time? Notice too, how many times things tumble or break when they are being handled with disrespect. And there are those times when we will persist over one inanimate obstacle after another—obstinately completing an action that we later regret. Has anybody not experienced the piece of malfunctioning equipment that "cures" itself when confronted with a technician or repairman? Maybe it was angry at being mistreated and doesn't really need twiddling—just a little love and respect. Or maybe it was just being perverse—chuck it out.

Were matter in some form of intelligent interface with its surrounding environment, a lot of life's inexplicable synergy would be easier to accept and appreciate—though not necessarily to understand. With inbuilt intelligence, we could better comprehend that great mystery of chaos theory—the discovery that order and stability are able to arise naturally and spontaneously from within a complex system. A "complex system" is composed of an uncountable number of components, each acting independently and unpredictably. Examples would be a natural rain forest, a global weather system, the whirlpool in a stream, a sandy beach, a natural community, or a spiralling galaxy. If the components of such a system are able to communicate and react at some level with each other, building intelligence from the bottom up, then the spontaneous arising of order and stability is not so inexplicable.

It may forever be beyond us to comprehend the nature of communications between matter, or to understand how matter accumulates and responds to knowledge of its vibrational world. Yet it is unlikely that our own animate bodies could build or maintain themselves were there not communication going on at the molecular level within. Just as all the life in the ocean depends upon the humble plankton for its survival, so might all the complex expressions of consciousness in Universe depend upon the simple intelligence of subatomic particles and light itself.

When we look at the bigger picture, it is clear that the long-term action takes place in the arena of the inanimate world. The fleeting lives of human beings, butterflies, and even giant redwood trees are overshadowed by the birth and unfolding of a mountain range or the slightest twist of the galaxy's spiral arm. If some intelligence did not exist within this inanimate backdrop, it is unlikely that the ingredients could ever have come together that enable it to exist within our own complex organism.

The four elements
they shape the cosmos

MUCH OF THIS book has been a voyage of discovery for your author, often prompted by earlier discoveries, realizations and serendipitous connections. In this chapter I begin by taking you through the thought processes leading to a rediscovery, for me, of something so basic that it's a bit embarrassing to admit. Aristotle knew about it, as have many since. But in case you have not explored the subject, it might help to see how I made my way to it.

As work progressed on the previous chapter, it seemed obvious that there were different categories of inanimate things. A first category would include static things like rocks and paperclips and plastic chairs. These were things that just sat there without any real movement or interacting parts.

The second category of inanimates would cover the things loosely grouped as machines, such as pianos, cars and computers, which involve lots of complexity and function. Top Silicon Valley figures now assure us that we will one day need a charter of rights for the machines they are developing.

The third and final category was to be those self-organizing inanimate phenomena that display some of the features of living organisms—such as movement, internal organization, consumption, and cyclical activity. This covered everything from oceans and rivers, to tornadoes and thunderclouds, to stars and swirling galaxies. They all seemed to be of a definite different category to rocks and chairs and computers. They could be called self-organizing inanimates.

The first difficulty was in deciding just where to draw lines. Was a sword, a lever or a pair of scissors to be in the static category with rocks, or classed with machines, once they are fashioned by us for a purpose? What category does a tree become when made into a table or a mill-wheel? It was all getting kind of fuzzy.

Inanimate objects are classified scientifically into three major categories - those that don't work, those that break down and those that get lost.

—RUSSELL BAKER

And I was having a problem with rocks, in that first grouping of things that just sat there doing nothing. What other items are there from the natural world that fit in this category? Soil is too organic and filled with microbes to be seen as inert or inanimate. The continental plates continually re-arrange themselves, floating above an active interior. All I could really come up with was different variations of rock—ranging in size from sand to mountains.

Surely there could not be a valid first category of inanimates that comprised thousands of man-made items such as plastic chairs and just one item from the natural world: rocks? Then what about the gigantic rocks that are mountains, which would better belong in the third, self-organizing category? Geologists tell us that mountain ranges develop from the plains in a dynamic and organized fashion and eventually fade away. The process, from start to finish, can take from 70 million to over a billion years. Sand too, can be part of a dynamic system, forming moving dunes with the wind of the desert and shifting beaches at the inter-face between land and ocean. And that sand may once have been a rock and before that part of the mountain. Are highly organized crystals in the same group as rocks? Some sort of rethink was definitely called for.

Eventually it dawned upon me that humans beings have only been on the planet for a geological blip, and that in a relatively short period of time all the stuff made by mankind will return to the category of everything else—to that from which they once came. Even the thousands of years that it will take for a plastic chair to return to earth represent less than a day in the lifespan of a mountain. Suddenly my perception of a neat little arrangement of inanimate categories started to fall apart.

This realization forced me to put those three groups back into the same pot, and I looked once again at my earlier listing of self-organizing inanimates. Many of the items on it seemed to be water-related, like rivers, oceans, glaciers, currents, snowflakes, clouds, springs, and geysers. Everything connected with water seemed to display self-organizational skills. In fact, I had earlier written a whole chapter on water, so well did it display the characteristics of intelligent behavior. You can find that at the back of these pages now, in the Afterwords.

The few things on my list of self-organizing inanimates that were not related to water were volcanoes, stars and fire. Of course, these were all fire-related and went on a different list, to which lightning was soon added. But it seemed to me that the list was not long enough and there was a sense that something was still missing. Before too long I saw the light, and realized that light itself is a manifestation of the fire in the heart of stars, and with it the entire electromagnetic spectrum of energy. This is the energy of the Sun's fire that is stored in plants and animals, and converted back to energy in our own intestines. Energy—what could we do without it? It makes life possible, and our skill at using it has enabled our civilization to develop.

At some point around here, it finally dawned upon me that half of the traditional Western four elements were staring me in the face. It is what science worked with before the Periodic Table took over. Most of us were once taught about the Periodic Table of Elements, which neatly groups all the chemical elements existing in this Universe, from hydrogen to uranium, by their atomic weights. I first heard of the Four Elements when being taught the Periodic Table in school; presented as the simplistic approach taken by ignorant and uninformed people before modern chemistry came along to enlighten us.

The Four Elements had always seemed of possible relevance, but I never really gave it a lot of thought. The Periodic Table is an inspired, essential, and reliable tool for science, arising from the brilliant discoveries of chemists, but the concept of four elements is neither born out of ignorance nor a blind spot for chemistry. It is a complementary approach, looking at different aspects of the same picture. It is another way of viewing things altogether and continues to play an important role in many Eastern therapies and spiritual practices, which often include a fifth element.

In addition to Fire and Water, the remaining two elements from the Western tradition are, of course, Earth and Air. The Earth element is, fundamentally, solid matter everywhere that has condensed throughout Universe. To us, it is the body of this planet from the bacteria-laden surface soil to the mystery at its core. By extension it also encompasses all those things arising from or extracted from it, from rocks to gold nuggets, plastic chairs to computers. Earth elements have a fixed form and solid structure. Unlike the other elements, they are less flowing and dynamic. Earth forms the material parts of living things such as herring, butterflies, and people, though they cannot come to animated life until combined with the other three elements.

Air embraces us and surrounds us, shielding life on this planet from the dangerous radiation of outer space and supplying it with the balanced levels of oxygen and carbon dioxide needed for survival. Air embodies music, allowing sound to travel through its body. Air delivers information to our nose in the form of smells. Air self-organizes into winds, tornadoes, and hurricanes throughout the solar system and not just in the specific climatic conditions found on Earth. Air embodies our entire atmosphere, with its global cycles carrying both the moisture of water and the heat of Sun around the planet.

The stable atmosphere appears to be a complex and self-governing phenomenon, complete with high-altitude jet streams and lower winds, which come and go with seasonal regularity. It maintains the average temperatures to which we had, until recently, grown accustomed, and no one has really figured out just how our atmosphere has managed to keep the balance of gases right for our existence. It is a most impressive feat, involving cooperation with blooms of algae in the oceans that can be the size of Britain. Too late perhaps, we are recognizing the unsettling climatic effects of our own thoughtless attitude to the element of Air.

Air would embody the gas planet Jupiter, and the swirling activity of its complex atmosphere and collections of rings. Air might even embrace the clouds of interstellar dust, and play some part in their conversion into the fire of burning stars.

And now, looking at four primal categories, it became clear that there was relevance to this idea, developed by the ancient Greeks. Earth, Air, Fire and Water—the Four Elements. Everything started to make sense, and now a new dedicated chapter was required—since the Four Elements embody the animate world as well as the inanimate. Empedocles is the one credited with first putting the Four Elements into words, though the concept long predated him in the East. This philosopher, healer and scientist of the 5th century B.C. described the spiritual essence of the elements, as well as their material nature.

During the same period, Democritus proposed that all matter is composed of infinitesimally tiny atoms which themselves vary in characteristics, thus explaining the physical properties of the world. Aristotle and Plato favored the Four Elements though Aristotle held with some tenets of the atomists. As is so often the case, one theory needed to prevail upon the other and it is now assumed that the atomists won out over those who favored the concept of the Four Elements. Yet when spirit is brought into the equation, we can see that the theories need not be antagonistic. The principle of Four Elements can be seen as describing four fundamental types of spirit at play in the world, defining aspects of matter that are not a part of its physical makeup. The element of Fire does not even require matter in order to exist as light.

All the living animals and plants of the world are themselves combinations of these four basic elements. Our own breath of life depends on air, while the energy that powers us comes from the fire of Sun, stored in plants through photosynthesis. About 70 percent of our body is water and most of the dry remainder is derived from products of the earth, ingested as food. Perhaps organic life as we know it can only exist when all four elements are at play. Perhaps it will always come into being when all four are at play. And without space, the fifth element of Buddhist philosophy, there would be no arena for the four elements to play within. They wisely incorporate space (the Void) into the equation, as does Hindu philosophy.

The Four Elements themselves live in an eternal dance as they continue to shape this cosmos and its subcomponents from nothing more than its original elemental clouds of thin gas. While this chapter arose as the result of my efforts to find categories of the inanimate, it became increasingly clear that, looking at the "big picture," it is a little arrogant to even distinguish the animate from the inanimate. All the varieties of animal and plant life on this planet are but more combinations of the same Four Elements that make it up, representing but a tiny fraction of the total planet's matter content, and an infinitesimal fraction of the greater Universe's elemental content. In this setting, we human beings struggle to explain the workings of this living cosmos, hampered by the assumption that organic life, ours specifically, is the only vessel of intelligence within its embrace.

Free will: no human preserve
even a grain of sand might have it

SOME YEARS AGO I met John Walsh, a man who had perfected a microscope-cum-camera that was able to follow individual microorganisms, using a clever combination of both hands and both feet to operate the tracking, focus, camera, and zoom. I was surprised when he told me that, as he tracked different members of the same microscopic species of rotifer, he noticed that they had quite distinctive tastes—what appeared to be personal likes and dislikes. Some of them would avoid eating the ever-present algae, while most would include it, as did the happy little guy opposite. His examination of food cavities within different members of the single-celled protozoan, called Stentor, gave him the impression that they, too, had distinctly varied tastes.

Walsh also recalled once being surprised during feeding trials with laboratory-bred rats, to find that some of them loved Mars bars while others would not touch them.

It is ironic that mankind should perceive "free will" as a solely human preserve, when we determinedly attempt to eliminate it from our structured lives as much as possible. Most wild animals and even microbes would appear to be making free will choices every moment of their lives. Some of the experiments of quantum mechanics suggest that even electrons are capable of this. It is unlikely that many animals even have a concept of "time off" when they get to "do their own thing" and enjoy

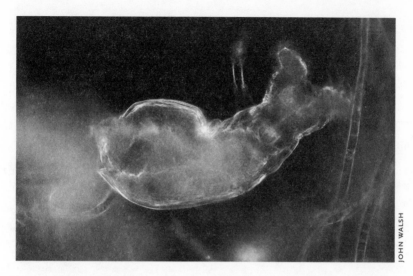

JOHN WALSH

life. I reckon most of them enjoy it most of the time, except during occasional brushes with danger and times of extreme hunger.

Let us imagine that we are surveying what a hundred people had for dinner in the United States last night. Most would have had flesh, and most of that would have been beef, pork, chicken, or fish. Some milk product or egg will be included and most else would be derived from wheat, corn, soybeans, and half a dozen basic vegetables—potato, onion, tomato, carrot, lettuce, peppers. Excluding spices and seasoning, that's about fifteen foods making up a large majority of the diet of the United States—plus chemicals, sugar, and drugs such as coffee, alcohol, and cola drinks.

Certainly a small but growing number of North Americans may be moving towards more natural foods and a more diverse diet. Still, we might well find that there is more edible variety for an amoeba within a jam jar of pond water than there is on the menu of the average American fast food outlet.

How can we think that the average American's choice of McDonald's over Kentucky Fried Chicken is a representation of free will and decide that the amoeba is simply following instincts—exhibiting programmed behavior over which it has no control? Consider too, that the free will of the amoeba is not subjected to a daily barrage of advertising seeking to channel its will to that of some particular corporation.

When a fox, pigeon, or salmon chooses to cross an international boundary it need not make plans in advance, and is unlikely to be aware of the geopolitical significance of its route. This is in stark contrast to human beings, whose free will of movement on the planet's surface is increasingly restricted by passports, visas, baggage checks, and other controls—done for our protection, we are told. Increasingly, we are forced to behave like sheep in order to travel from A to B on planet Earth.

Most of those in today's employed world have little opportunity to exercise much free will during their working week. It could be said that many human beings lack the flexibility of the average wild animal, which may have developed a routine in its life but has done so without the need for clocks or complex regulations and legislation. Though the blackbird couple in my garden routinely bring new blackbirds into being, their daily flitting around the garden and rooftop, their singing and their eating patterns all develop according to each day rather than to any schedule beyond singing in the morning's early rays.

Perhaps all of this planet's creatures exhibit free will of one form or another. Their freedom of choice is probably a key factor behind the natural stability that chaos theory recognizes in stable communities and natural phenomena. The more we study the behaviour of the natural world, the more it appears as though individual choice is exercised regularly by dogs, fish, worms and amoebas, as well as by people.

Perhaps free will extends to the plant world also, where early choices about the placement of root and branch development are essential ingredients in the quest for life. Plants love to live. Time lapse photography, speeding up a month of a plant's life into minutes, shows this clearly as seedlings and growing plants burst, shoot, writhe, ravel, and wrap themselves in a frantic frenzy to make greater contact with the life-giving Sun above. Although we have no means of subterranean photography, we can assume that the same dynamic quest is going on below the surface as the roots reach into Mother Earth seeking water, foundation and nutrients. There is no sound scientific basis for assuming that the fiendishly clever life-preserving features of the plant world have been arrived at wholly by accident—it is simply declared unscientific to think otherwise.

We may struggle to empathize with the struggles that an ancient tree has undergone within its lifetime—a lifetime which may have begun when the Buddha was still alive. We do know that it was but one seed in millions that managed to beat the incredible odds of first sprouting, and then growing to full maturity. We cannot assume that, for plants, survival is purely determined by the chance of weather, wind, and random genetics. In nature, some seeds sprout and survive while the vast majority die in the struggle. Perhaps the success of an ancient tree in the wild involved not only the factor of chance, but also an element of making the smarter free will choices during its life?

Perhaps our own body parts and cells rely upon an element of free will. There is no central director telling each skin cell when to divide, managing our digestion or directing the path of a blood cell. Every human cell is a miniature complex system of its own, containing countless millions of individual components moving around within a single outer membrane. Included within the cell wall are up to 30,000 different types of proteins, configured as organelles, ligands, ribosomes, enzymes, endosomes, DNA, and others.

Each cell is a veritable factory with more parts than there are people in a large city. It must feed itself, rebuild internal bits, excrete waste, respond to numerous external stimuli, create bioelectricity, and decide when to divide and when to die. And when it divides, it is able to replicate each of its many components, including all the 3.1 billion DNA base pairs of the double helix. All this is taking place within a cell that could share the head of a pin with 10,000 other cells.

There is no manager or controller within an individual cell, coordinating the activities of its millions of components. They work it out for themselves, and the more that we discover about cells the more unlikely it seems that they could be functioning by accident and chance alone. Is there free will going on within this tiny space? Without an element of free will, it is difficult to see how there would be anything at all going on. It would be total chaos, or more accurately, disorder.

When working on the Four Elements chapter, it seemed apparent that an element of free will, albeit of a different nature, is at play in the development of form and structure within the inanimate world, from winding rivers to spiralling galaxies. For thousands of years our ancestors practiced rituals designed to influence the free will of the rain clouds and Sun, or to beg favors and support from springs and other natural formations. Sometimes we seem to witness free will manifesting amongst the more mundane elements of the inanimate world, when everyday objects and phenomenon appear to have a mind of their own—in situations usually dismissed as amazing coincidence.

Now seems like a good time to come back to those grains of sand we left in the chapter on consciousness, having been to Sun and all over the place since. Free will? I find it difficult to think of a grain of sand as having free will, so far away from it am I in the scale of existence. But I will make a case for it anyway.

Countless trillions of molecules combine to create a grain of sand, with every grain differing slightly from all others so that, at the subtlest level, each would have its own unique energetic signature. Could it be that, in the thrust of the surf and the wind, each grain is savoring its time in the action and bright lights at the top of the beach or dune?

At the tumbling edge of the ocean's surf no amount of computing power could accurately predict the location of a churning grain of sand 10 seconds into its future. Perhaps each grain of sand exerts some play, however infinitesimal, in the tumbling trajectories and flows of its occasionally action-packed existence. The sand might be electromagnetically "in touch" with the molecules of water, and the other grains of sand surrounding it. Atomic particles themselves seem able to affect each other's behavior, so we must ask whether this ability is also at play in the larger constructs that they form, like grains of sand? This contact may be affecting the outcome of the interaction between sand and water, and representing an expression of free will.

Life is like a game of cards. The hand you are dealt is determinism; the way you play it is free will.
—JAWAHARLAL NEHRU

And there are the singing sand dunes, first reported to the West by Marco Polo, that have been noted in some thirty-five locations around the world. Some individual dunes are known to burst into "song" twice daily and with some regularity. The sound can easily be heard over a kilometer away and continues to provoke debate amongst scientists as to the cause.

Going down a level from grains of sand, we find that two mathematicians from Princeton have proved the Free Will Theorem, which suggests that even quantum particles might exhibit free will. To put it simply, Professors Simon Kochen and John Conway demonstrated that if particles do not have free will, then neither could people. Conversely, if people do exercise free will, then the same is true of particles. Conway said, "If you really take free will seriously, the universe is full of it." Another way of expressing the meaning of this proof is to say that unless atomic particles themselves have free will, then everything we do and think and say, every single word I write upon this page, has been an inevitable consequence of the unique and specific arrangement of particles existing immediately after the Big Bang.

To see a World in a Grain of Sand
And a Heaven in a Wild Flower,
Hold Infinity in the palm of your hand
And Eternity in an hour.
—WILLIAM BLAKE

Feedback
it makes the world go 'round

W ERE IT NOT for feedback, your grocer would just run out of bread and nobody would ever bother to bake any more, let alone deliver it to the store. Just as well, since without any feedback you'd never get hungry again anyway. Everything that happens in this world prompts something else to respond, and will then react to that response, and those exchanges will have an effect upon all else that is in the mix.

The climate that sucks up moisture from the planet, drying up oceans, rivers, lakes and land surface, will eventually send it back to Earth as drops of liquid rain, hard balls of hail, or fluffy crystal snowflakes. Weather distributes the water that sprouts seeds, feeding the forests and savannahs they produce. Weather slowly wears down mountains with its winds. The planet's weather system is the self-organized totality of countless giant and miniature feedback systems looping into each other across the planet. It represents the totality of all the environmental exchanges taking place on planet Earth, from a hurricane sucking up the ocean to a jogger panting in the park.

We live in a world in which everything is continually reacting freely with everything else. Feedback loops just go on and on—every action affecting every future action. A listener's raised eyebrow informs the speaker of question or dissention. That clinking sound tells you you've dropped your keys, the painful squeal that you're on the dog's tail.

You jump away—feedback loops back and forth. A "thank you" tells the giver a gift was worth the effort. Appreciation feels good. Feedback loops back and forth, connecting us all together.

Feedback makes our world work. Life would be quite impossible without it. We can see how badly things go wrong when it is forcibly removed from the picture. These consequences are covered in my previous book, *Uncommon Sense—The State is Out of Date*. In it we discover what happens when, for instance, the government breaks the feedback loop between eaters and farmers. The state determines what farmers should grow and how much it should cost and then passes regulations to replace the buying decisions that would otherwise have been fed back by food consumers. We are familiar by now with the results: diseased animals, bloody culls, food mountains, bankrupt farmers, fraud, corruption, a junk-food diet, and more dangerous chemicals in the food chain. All this, served up with the accompaniment of cover-ups and bland assurances from those responsible. This is one example of the mayhem that is created when feedback is blocked.

Your every response to the stimuli of your surroundings not only determines the future path of your life, but that of the society in which you live. The critical effects of minor actions may often show no perceivable link between that action and the eventual unfolding of future events that were subtly influenced. Sometimes, on the other hand, the connection will be blindingly obvious.

The chapter "Organized Religion" was followed by the one tenet all belief systems agree on—the Golden Rule. This advises us not to do things unto others that we would not wish upon ourselves—though the Christian version leaves out the nots. This general tenet could be the most valuable consideration to make as we respond in the vital feedback loop that forms our relationship with others in this world. It is basically about empathy—the ability to feel "inside" other people and have an idea of what is going on in their world.

The arguments in support of a community incorporating empathy into their dealings with one another seem transparently obvious. Yet when we look about us, an appreciation of this principle is clearly lacking in today's civilization. Increasingly, legislation and the rule of law are replacing the natural foundation of social order that arises from living in a community of people with freely flowing feedback. Today, whether an action is legal or illegal is the only consideration that many feel constrained to take when conducting their affairs with others. This has not had a beneficial effect upon the core morality of our society.

Bearing in mind our diminished level of empathy for others in human social interchanges, it is no surprise that there is another entire level of feedback that is very rarely considered or thought to be relevant. This is the feedback between us and the non-human features of the environment with which we interact. As bioelectrically driven organisms, we are believed to carry and project some small electromagnetic field around with us. This field may form a subtle feedback loop with our environment, as the electrons present in all matter pick up on the electromagnetic vibrations of our very presence. This could incorporate what is often referred to as the "aura"—a surrounding field of light that is visible to some, though invisible to most of us. It is a part of the "vibe" that we put out, and may account for more than we imagine.

The Golden Rule, useful in many situations of life, may let us down when we try to empathize with what we would have done, or not done, to us in our interactions with worms, hills, trees, oceans, or cooking pots when we are "doing" things to them. But the principle of respect and the feedback of gratitude can do us no harm, and may just reap rewards in our ongoing association with the many other aspects of this creation. Nobody and, indeed, no thing benefits from being treated with disrespect.

Respect and gratitude to the world around us is not a new idea. Before the arrival of organized religions it was almost universally the practice to express gratitude and respect to the natural world and its special features, as well as to beings of pure spirit. There were thousands of different ways of doing this, with countless variations around the world. Entities were addressed to thank Earth and its waters and the fire and the wind and both general and specific sources of food. Blessings and thanks usually accompanied the killing of animals for meat. Many of these practices were subsequently integrated into and modified by the mass-market religions that came to dominate spiritual behaviour.

There was far more feedback going on in the past than we see today, and showing this respect was held to be connected with how well life treated us. We are taught to laugh at such notions as being primitive superstition. In our world we are expected to live by a cultural and scientific doctrine explaining the rest of the Universe as an unconscious accidental occurrence of some sort. We are not expected to recognize any faculty in plants or inanimate phenomena that is able to recognize and respond to our feedback of gratitude or respect.

> *Forget not that the earth delights to feel your bare feet*
> *and the winds long to play with your hair.*
> **—KAHLIL GIBRAN,** *THE PROPHET*

Perhaps all the effort that primitive men and women put into saying "thank you" for the blessings of life was not a total waste of time. This sort of "superstitious" behavior went on for thousands of years and just might have been sustained for so long because people noticed the difference that it made to their lives and to the world around them.

Even if our world were not in such a mess today, it would be arrogant to assume that those who came before us were so dumb as to persist in attempted feedback with unresponsive co-respondents for thousands of years if there were no benefits. I have certainly noticed the difference it makes in my life. Simple appreciation for and awareness of what I am doing establishes a better connection with all else involved, whether I am shopping, cooking, or driving a vehicle. This feedback of consciousness makes a difference and things will go better, taste better, flow better . . . most of the time.

Gratitude is good, whatever lies at the receiving end. Of course, we should not let ritualized gratitude detract from the enjoyment of that for which we are being grateful, since that enjoyment is probably the best feedback we can give.

We are in a one-to-one relationship with our Universe. We do well to treat the rest of this world with the respect it deserves—it is a fellow part of the Universal organism to which we all belong. "All is One" excludes neither the galaxies nor the grains of sand, whilst including us. We should strive to make respectful choices that we will not regret, regardless of where they lead us. Every action in our life constitutes a part of the intricate feedback loop that defines both us and our relationship with the world. Respect the rest of You.

The biggest question
we'll never answer this

T HE BIGGEST QUESTION we can ask must be: Why does anything exist? Why is there even energy, let alone a Universe complete with galaxies, black holes, stars, planets, oceans, human beings, trees, and grains of sand?

We can safely assume that the answer to this fundamental question will always remain a mystery. And we can be grateful that we are not in the paradoxical position of posing the opposite question: Why isn't there anything?

As you can perhaps deduce from chapter size, although this is the biggest question we can ask, it is not the most important.

From the bottom up
creation as a built-in feature

THOUGH $E = MC^2$ must be the most familiar equation on the planet, it is also the strangest one and the most difficult to truly grasp, regardless of whether you are a fisherman or a physicist. In a nutshell, the formula tells us that energy and matter are different manifestations of the same thing—that they share equivalence, or relativity. This is, as Einstein put it mildly, "a somewhat unfamiliar conception for the average mind." The mechanics of it are simple, though—the energy equivalence of an item (E) is equal to its mass (m) multiplied by the speed of light (c) squared, which is an exceedingly large number.[21]

Our usual reference to $E = mc^2$ is in terms of its ability to tell us how much energy will be released by matter in a nuclear explosion. The first atomic bombs, dropped on Japanese cities, provided graphic proof that Einstein's formula was correct and prompted him to quip that he wished he had become a watchmaker instead of a physicist.

Any matter, iron or daffodils, would share the same per-kilo bang power as the uranium that is converted in a nuclear explosion, if it were possible to effect its conversion to energy.[22] But we seem to always look at the famous formula in terms of the energy released through explosively disassembling matter. It is hardly surprising that we do, considering how much we identify with our material world, living in a culture focused on conflict and mass destruction.

For a change, let us look at Einstein's equation from the other way around entirely—constructively. If there were a means by which energy could be converted into matter, then how much energy would be required to create a certain amount of matter? Let us look at a small amount of matter—the 110 grams of hydrogen within 1,000 grams (1 liter) of water—the H in the H2O. This little bit of hydrogen has been in existence since the beginnings of our Universe, and when we apply Einstein's formula it turns out to have a huge energy equivalence, exceeding that of the atom bomb that devastated Hiroshima—by 150 times!

It seems astounding to us that so much energy would be needed to create such a little amount of matter, were such a feat possible. But it becomes more believable when we consider that when those 110 grams of hydrogen atoms first marked territory in the cosmos as a pre-stellar cloud of dust, they took up more space than they do now, in that liter of water. Distributed at about one atom per cubic centimeter, they would have occupied a cloud that had three times the volume of the moon.

Water = bombs worksheet: $E = mc^2$
$m = 0.110$ kilo (110 grams of hydrogen)
$c^2 = 90{,}000{,}000{,}000{,}000{,}000$
$E = 9{,}900{,}000{,}000{,}000{,}000$ joules
1 kiloton of energy $= 4{,}190{,}000{,}000{,}000$ joules
$9{,}900{,}000{,}000{,}000{,}000$ joules $= 2{,}362$ kilotons
15 kilotons x 150 bombs $= 2{,}250$ kilotons

As much as we view matter in a matter-of-fact way it is truly remarkable stuff and has been upon an incredible journey of condensation, combination, and evolution on its way to becoming the world that we experience—or perhaps the world that it experiences as us and daffodils and clouds and stars.

We might consider it difficult to go back to the beginning of our Universe and try to guess at what exactly was going on when matter first appeared. We are still not sure about when and where the battle of Troy was fought, what the legend of Atlantis is all about, or who really shot President Kennedy. Yet with seemingly less evidence at hand, our top physicists are making intelligent guesses about just what had to happen from Universe's first billionth of a second onward in order for it to be where it is today, describing eras that occupied micro-seconds in a Universe smaller than a single atom.

Putting aside the very fuzzy question of just how and why it all started, it remains reasonable and, perhaps, relevant to be curious about one thing concerning the beginnings of the Universe. This is the question of *which came first, energy or matter?* Of course, they may have both suddenly arisen from nothing, from nothing at all. But let us consider the question.

Though matter and energy may share equivalence, they have different requirements for their existence. Matter lives with time by its side— it has a history with a starting point and changes as it passes through time. Matter has mass and substance and takes up space, and where that space is is where that substance exists. Because we humans are substance this all sounds perfectly obvious. But energy lives a very different life to matter, even though we both may share equivalence.

Photons, whether vibrating as light or other energy, have neither substance nor mass and with no volume they have no physical need of a place to exist. Its lack of substance enables light to be compressed in order to carry vast amounts of information through fiber-optic cables. There is uncertainty over whether photons actually travel from A to B (as in star to Earth) and whether the concept of space, as something to travel through, even exists from the photon's point of view. Could it be that energy does not actually need space in order to exist? Though we measure the distance to nearby star Sirius as 8.6 light years, for the time-free photons of light the journey is instantaneous. Perhaps from a photon's perspective the space between does not exist either, and everything is everywhere at once.

I do not believe that we have the traditional "chicken-or-egg" conundrum here. If there was a first between matter and energy, then it seems inescapably clear that energy is the only reasonable candidate to make a claim for first existence.

If energy did come first, we have a viable source for the matter that then came into being. Perhaps the so-called Big Bang took place when a truly inconceivable amount of energy was being condensed into matter. Perhaps it would be better termed the Big Whoosh, as it is the very opposite process to that which creates mankind's biggest bang—the nuclear explosion, in which a small amount of matter is converted into energy. But I am no physicist and apologize if the suggestion is preposterous, though it seems more reasonable than to believe that matter suddenly appeared from nothing, and was accompanied or followed by energy.

Jesus said, "If the flesh came into being because of spirit, it is a wonder. But if spirit came into being because of the body, it is a wonder of wonders. Indeed, I am amazed at how this great wealth has made its home in this poverty."

—GOSPEL OF THOMAS, 3RD CENTURY GNOSTIC SCROLLS
DISCOVERED IN 1945, NAG HAMMADI LIBRARY

But whichever came first, if there was a first, in "the beginning" matter materialized as subatomic particles and expanded rapidly into a newly created space. These particles soon self-assembled into atoms of hydrogen and helium, which then congregated in large thin clouds of matter separated by the vast emptiness of space. In these simple clouds lay all of the raw materials for today's Universe. At a fundamental level, there is nothing physically new in the Universe—just endless new arrangements of those original particles. The evolution of those original particles is every bit as important as biological evolution, fundamental to it, and possibly more difficult to "rationally" explain.

Having evolved rapidly into atoms and then assembled into clouds, the next great jump in particle evolution appears to have taken place within a few hundred million years, equivalent to a few years in the life of a 100-year-old Universe. It was then that these clouds of original atoms, each one a tiny parcel of condensed vibration, first managed to self-organize into complex bodies called stars. Yes, out of drifting clouds of thin hydrogen and helium gas, these particles self-assembled into massive fusion powered devices, encased in multiple layers of containment rotating at different speeds. Even with possible help from faint electromagnetic fields permeating the early Universe this is some achievement.

These newly formed stars both power, and are managed by, highly complicated and little understood electromagnetic fields extending into space well beyond their physical bodies. And just what is it that these stars happen to do? Their primary function appears to be the creation of new energy. That new energy is able to accomplish many things, such as: forging new elements out of simple hydrogen and helium; transmitting waves of energy deep into space; illuminating and maintaining a solar system; supporting life as we know it. If energy did precede matter, then it certainly looks as though there could be something of a reproductive nature going on here: energy condenses into simple matter, which soon thereafter forms itself into the ultimate energy-producing device—a burning star. Energy becomes matter, which begets energy.

Does it not seem just a little bit, well, blind to be pushing scientific theory past the point of credibility in the attempt to explain how randomly distributed thin clouds of gas, with only Newtonian principles at play, are able to self-organize into galaxies full of steadily burning stars?

Armed with Newton's principles, the knowledge of quantum physics and many billions invested in the highest technology of the day, our finest physicists are still striving to create power using the same principles employed by stars. Yet these same physicists display no embarrassment when they avow that accidental and unintelligent process was capable of bringing about this device "in the wild." I certainly hope that these top brains one day create a viable fusion powered nuclear plant, but doubt that it will run for billions of years without malfunction, maintenance or any external management.

Star formation would be somewhat easier to understand, though messier for scientific thinking, if we allowed for an intrinsic intelligence in matter itself—a subject explored earlier herein. The origin of this intelligence may have lain in the colossal amount of energy that condensed or converted into matter in the very first place. Energy, we have seen, is the basic force of this Universe. For us, it is energy that provides the spirit of life. Without energy we do not live or think. Without energy there is nothing that we call living left. Yet we are brought up with the assumption that it is us who gives the life to energy, and not the other way around.

Science recognizes four fundamental forces at play in the Universe. Two of them are gravity and electromagnetic energy (as in light), which we can feel and see, so to speak. They have an enormous impact upon our world and we are very aware of them, even though gravity was unknown before Newton. The other two are called the strong nuclear force and the weak nuclear force. Though they also have a major impact upon our world, we know almost nothing about them, other than that they must exist, whatever they are. They are names given to unexplained and fundamental factors at play in the subatomic world, without which atoms of matter would be unable to hold together and quarks would be unable to change flavor. Don't ask.

Many of the experiments of quantum physics have given glimpses of what those unfettered by tradition might interpret as intelligent behaviour by particles. If quanta of energy do, indeed, exhibit or facilitate intelligence, then perhaps when an unimaginable quantity of quanta originally condensed into matter an element of intelligence would have been retained. And this elemental intelligence may have remained in place during the hydrogen's assembly into an energy-producing star. And have stayed there when its atoms ended up on Earth enjoined with oxygen to make water, or with carbon to make wood. *Indeed, this intelligence may have played a part in the process.*

Intelligence, at a fundamental level, makes more sense when we consider it organizing from the bottom up. We recognize that a school of fish, a termite colony, a rainforest, and planet Earth display some of the characteristics of single functioning organisms. We accept that the school's and termite colony's coordination somehow arises as a bottom-up composite of the multitude of individual fish and termite brains, though we do not understand this type of intelligence. Chaos theory recognizes the order and harmony that arise within complex systems such as a rainforest and planet Earth, though does not officially recognize it as intelligence.

Were an elemental intelligence innate to matter it becomes more credible that huge clouds of thin gas can develop into stars, whatever natural laws and forces are harnessed in the process; that oceans create defined rivers within themselves; that weather systems develop into organized (and once-predictable) patterns. Built-in bottom-up intelligence would help explain the ongoing order and incredibly clever structures that arise in evolving worlds, however long it may take to develop a mountain range, a stable weather system or Saturn's rings and their shepherding moons.

Intelligence may have occurred to quantum physicist David Bohm when, more than 60 years ago, he witnessed free electrons organizing themselves in a plasma soup and is said to have described them as displaying mind-like properties. From this elemental perspective we do not have a super overseeing intelligence planning everything in detail, but a bottom-up intelligence that enables things to evolve useful properties and forms as circumstances provoke. Perhaps intelligence just is, in the same intangible way that gravity just is—or consciousness.

One of the most difficult types of intelligence for our rational intelligence to understand is, ironically, our own, based as it is upon the free interaction of hundreds of billions of independent neurons distributed throughout our brain. They organize and make associations with whatever other neurons they choose and nowhere is there any sign of central control.

If we cannot even understand our own process of intelligence, how can we be expected to understand how trillions upon trillions of drifting hydrogen and helium atoms in a pre-stellar cloud managed to engineer their own amazing feat of star formation? But they did it, as we and a bright Universe are able to witness. It is time to acknowledge other vehicles of intelligence that are beyond our comprehension, and not just the incomprehensible version that we personally experience and accept.

We struggle to imagine any single entity clever enough to engineer and implement something as amazing as a blazing star or as complex as a simple sparrow. The specific design of a versatile carbon atom seems as unlikely to have been premeditated as it is to have been accidental. Could self-design be taking place? We see it in the complex structure and efficiency of an ant colony, where no single ant contains or directs the intelligence of the colony. We see it in a thundercloud where no single water molecule, or even a regular clique of them, decides just when to loose the lightning. No single neuron or set of them controls our brain; no single carbon atom shapes the diamond; no single sardine leads the school.

It is when the sub-components of intelligence are brought together that their interactions are able to bring about structure and form. Were a divine designer behind creation then we need not have waited so long for stars to form from clouds of dust, or for jellyfish to evolve into things like us. Yet were we to have waited for accidental process to stumble across a star, or us, it is likely that we would be waiting longer than forever.

Perhaps gOd, who is this Universe, began life itself as a simple entity swathed in clouds of dark thin gas, as unaware as a tiny fetus of that which it was to become. Some 14 billion years later, that baby has evolved into a massive mature organism—filled with star-stuffed galaxies, supernovas, quasars, planets, people, and many other strange unusual folk. So many different manifestations of matter have arisen through the evolution and combination of those initial subatomic particles, from sardines to iPods, from snowflakes to stars.

This Universe is, I would suggest, assembling and utilizing the vibration and intelligence of its myriad individual components and synthesizing them into a unified universal intelligence—a single mind. Whatever the nature of such a Universal Being at the beginning of time, it is now infinitely more substantial, evolved, enlightened and enlightening than was the infant Universe. And we are all playing a part in that cosmic evolution—every star-studded galaxy, each planet, person, butterfly, microbe, and molecule of Us that has the honour to exist—to be. Enjoy, appreciate, care.

Overview
wrapping it up

WHAT HAS BEEN the purpose of this book? My initial zeal was fuelled by a desire to re-open the lid on a very ancient subject—Sun. Many people have given voice to the concept that Sun is a conscious entity of some sort, but few today have explored the idea in much depth. Jews, Christians, and Muslims from Abraham onwards have shunned the idea of Sun being any sort of conscious entity, let alone a gOd. To embrace this idea was, perhaps, the ultimate heresy. For many centuries simply holding some of the beliefs put forward in these pages was punishable by execution, often in flames. In some countries today, they would still be considered dangerous. This sort of entrenched attitude by the status quo, over an extended period, has undoubtedly had a profound effect upon our thinking processes as a culture.

In the writing of this book, I have come across many brilliantly expounded propositions by others, conveying many of the concepts contained within these pages. I was surprised and delighted to discover how many of these "far out" ideas had already been embraced, both in the past and in current thinking. One can find abundant writing, often more knowledgeable than mine, on the living "Gaia" nature of this planet; on the consciousness of the Universe; and on the strangely intelligent behavior of subatomic particles. But serious recognition or consideration of Sun's consciousness is scant, without which it is difficult to integrate the bigger picture. Sun, after all, is for us the most influential character in that picture. The cultural control of obsolete religions is still working its effect upon our science and culture. It is high time that we break out of this mental straightjacket.

Thinking about Sun, and considering the power and consequences of its consciousness, inevitably led me via other stars and galaxies to the ultimate consciousness of the Universe itself. As I began to look into the nature of the predominant solar product, light, it became apparent that this all-pervasive fundamental force of the cosmos is a very important part of the picture, perhaps the most important part. Photons are the most fascinating and enigmatic particles of the quantum world, having neither mass nor substance, while possessing the ability to hold and convey energy and information. Whatever I learned about quantum physics intrigued me, and resonated with thoughts I had long held about the innate intelligence potential of inanimate matter, from paperclips to thunder clouds to stars.

Early on in the writing, it became obvious that I was straying into areas that religions have sought to define, even though my own upbringing had been completely devoid of religious education. A quick crash-course on world religions followed, revealing significant similarities between Zoroastrianism and the three Abraham-based religions that dominate so many of the world's cultures. The former worships Sun as a primary god who represents a supreme deity of light, whilst the latter worship an invisible supreme deity who dispenses a lot of light, and in whose image we are formed. Other important religions, such as Hinduism, Shinto, and Tibetan Buddhism have not abandoned or suppressed the animist beliefs at the roots of all religion, and seem not to have developed a taste for conquest in the name of their faith. It seemed relevant to write a few chapters attempting to summarize religions from, as I put it, an alien's point of view. Hopefully they were not tedious for you or, heaven forbid, offensive.

The value of a book like this is often measured by what readers receive from it—how can these ideas and information be used to improve lives? Perhaps the most fundamental understanding to gain is the importance of respect and appreciation for all the other factors of this world that interact with our lives, whether they be human, animal, vegetable, mineral or spirit. Usually, we give consideration only to our interactions with other human beings, and too frequently ignore even this when in pursuit of material success as defined by personal wealth and influence. We forget, or fail to realize, that the only true measure of success—our level of happiness and inner peace—is substantially affected by the quality of our interactions with all the others that share our world.

An indirect benefit to be gained from this book is a greater facility to understand the mechanisms and underlying principles at work in some of the once-thought-wacky beliefs that used to be the reserve of hippies and New Agers. Of course, astrology predates hippies by thousands of years, and herbs and products of the Earth were in every doctor's toolkit up to a century ago (when we didn't need a word for organically grown).

Many areas of traditional knowledge, based on generations of experience and wise observation, have been abandoned or lost altogether because their conclusions were offensive to the prevailing school of scientific thought, which believes adamantly in a mechanical and unconscious Universe. But many sources of knowledge are being rediscovered as interest grows in alternatives to mechanistic medicine and the corporate culture of the pharmaceutical industry.

The process of rediscovery is supported by sensitive new technologies enabling us to detect and influence delicate vibrational fields and currents that were once undetectable. Most Western scientists still dismiss such technologies as silly nonsense. Far Eastern scientists, not imprinted by Christianity, have no qualms about the study of spirit—subtle energy fields that extend beyond the physical body of matter, whether that matter be crystal, tree or human being.

Six years into this book, the whole Intelligent Design vs. Evolution story was going off big-time with lawyers and conflict and lots of headlines. After reading the positions of both sides, I couldn't help thinking that each side of the argument seemed as blinkered and chained to their positions as the other. It was high time that another option was thrown into the current either/or debate. Intelligence from the bottom up is that other option—a system in which everything, from a molecule of water to a neuron in our brain to Sun itself, is a part of the bottom that is subtly steering a greater whole.

On a broader level, what I hope to have imparted to readers is a clearer set of spectacles through which to view the world and the greater Universe. Although it would be beyond me to put these ideas forward in a scholarly manner, I have not strayed too far from logic, nor put forward many propositions that have not been propounded already—often by scholars. I have sought to interweave many of these ideas into a joined-up and coherent view of the miraculous cosmos in which we co-exist, providing a more all-embracing way of looking at our world. The purpose of this writing is not to simply tell you of what I have seen through these spectacles, but to enable you to see all of that, and more, yourself.

Afterwords

·

T HERE FOLLOW eight "Afterwords" that flow from the body of this book and deepen its understanding. Enjoy...

Smart evolution
and the roots of this book

DARWIN DISCOVERED the slow sequence of evolution-ary change. He was able to first spot, and then plot, the myriad of small changes leading upwards from simple creatures of the sea to more complex higher mammals. Nobody had previously considered that we might share ancestry with jellyfish, mice, and cabbages. It was a brilliant accomplishment. But the assumption that evolution is a random process is not proven by the fact that it can be interpreted as a sequence of accidental selections that were best suited to survival.

Of course the most suitably adapted new variations of a species survived best, but we do not know that their variety was arrived at by accident and without intention. Even Charles Darwin did not make the assumption of accidental change that is embraced by modern Darwinists. But that assumption fits best with today's prevailing belief that intelligence can only occur with conscious participation of brains similar to our own—preferably formally educated.

Can evolution explain the strange striped pattern of the zebra? As we know, the distinctive design of an individual zebra becomes a confusing array of unfamiliar stripes to a predator of the fleeing herd. This makes zebra stripes beneficial to survival. Had a handful of zebras accidentally developed distinctive stripes in the early evolution of the species, they would have stood out from the herd and been easier prey. Might the whole species have taken this route as a group strategy, utilizing some form of intelligence that Darwinists seek to deny?

Charles Fort's guide to Darwinism:
The fittest survive.
What is meant by the fittest?
Not the strongest; not the cleverest.
Weakness and stupidity everywhere survive.
There is no way of determining fitness except in that a thing does survive.
'Fitness', then, is only another name for 'survival.'
Darwinism: The survivors survive.

—FROM **BOOK OF THE DAMNED**, 1919

Darwinists assume that there is always a logical explanation that does not rely upon intelligence, but however clear the explanation, it cannot logically disprove the involvement of intelligence. The celebrated astronomer Sir Fred Hoyle pointed out that though it is scientifically possible for bacteria to have evolved accidentally out of the "chemical soup," the accomplishment would be tantamount to a random tornado assembling a jumbo jet from the disassembled parts resting in a junkyard it tears through. It once again brings to mind the old story about infinite monkeys with infinite time and typewriters coming out with the complete works of William Shakespeare, which is about as likely as one in an infinity of tornadoes assembling the jet cockpit correctly.

In many cases, science has demonstrated how it is conceivable that a series of random selections could have brought each species to its current condition. But however copious and specific their data, it does not disprove the possibility that either the innate intelligence in the organism itself, or that of some intangible group spirit, also plays a part in driving this genetic change.

We forget just how intelligent we were before we even had a brain, when two single cells set off on a journey of reproduction. In 9 months they managed to craft the entire organism known as a human being without any need for human intervention, so to speak. Limbs and internal organs were formed, with nerve connections to our brain and a circulatory system able to deliver fresh blood to every single cell in our body.

The meter-long strand of DNA within every cell of our body provides only a blueprint, and does not serve as the builder or engineer of the body. It takes up less than 1 percent of the cell's volume, sharing it with countless millions of other functioning components. Each cell is itself a small city, and each time it doubles so do each of those millions of individual components.

Our whole body is protected by a built in defense system featuring various specialized cells such as macrophages, which hunt and destroy invading bacteria, and T-Helper cells which co-ordinate and support the defending cells. These cells rally the appropriate defences when required, remembering strategies that worked for previous battles with invaders. They develop our body's resistance to disease. All this is delivered, together with incredible devices of digestion, and filtration systems beyond anything that science could mimic.

As intelligent as we think we have become, our dumb unthinking body is smart enough to put most of its vital features beyond our "intelligent" control processes—such as breathing, digestion, heartbeat, hunger, sleep, and so on. Though the progression from amoeba to flatworm to human being was a slow and incremental process, can all this have arisen by sheer chance, with no form of intelligence involved at all? Or might countless billions of cells in a self-organizing system be manifesting a form of group intelligence?

Perhaps the considerable built-in management intelligence of an organism would be cognizant of what has been happening to the organism it has run for the last 16 to 60 years. And perhaps the nature of this information is going to help determine the nature of any evolutionary changes in genetic code that are being passed on to the next generation. Naturally, different individual organisms will experiment with different change strategies and some will be more successful than others. And there will be an element of dice involved. Nothing in evolutionary science demonstrates that genetic change is a fully random process, just that it could be. Could it ever be that a family gifted with piano playing genes acquired these not accidentally, but from an ancestor who once learned to play and love the music of the piano to such an extent that a genetic imprint was crafted?

This chapter began while I was marooned for a week in a transit hotel at Bombay airport, scribbling away by the poolside in search of an idea for a book to follow *Uncommon Sense*. One of those ideas was about the inner intelligence of evolution, and I decided to go ahead with it. As the writing progressed beyond the piano player bit, things began to digress into serious topic drift. Among other topics, I strayed into the diet of an amoeba versus that of the average American, nanotechnology, Lovelock's Gaia, the Big Bang, Solar worship, and the consciousness of Sun. I had always thought Sun to be somehow conscious, but had never pursued that train of thought. As I did, and read more about Sun, I realized the real direction that this book would take—initially, at least. In any event, I have since discovered that pursuing this intelligent evolution thing would have laid me open to accusations of Lamarckism[23], heaven forbid!

I'm not completely sure how much this chapter now fits, but in the circumstances think this taste of it must be included. Perhaps, with further research into it, I would have ended up agreeing with Charles Darwin, whose own proposals were far less absolute than those of modern Darwinists. And perhaps I would have discovered how zebras got their stripes.

The little things of life
small rules the world

WITHOUT OUR earliest ancestors, the bacteria and other microbes, there could be no other life on this planet. They were the original life form to inhabit this Earth, possibly having begun their own evolution on a distant world. Unlike all other living organisms, they seem able to survive without all the Four Elements being present (earth, fire, water, and air). They are essential to our own existence and responsible for creating and managing the environment that sustains us.

We are inseparable from the bacteria within our bodies, most of which are providing essential services. Though not the case with grains of sand, if we could count the total bacteria on this planet they might even outnumber the stars in Universe. Understandably, we tend to know primarily about the bacteria that are either harmful or helpful to us. But the "bugs" that we fear and the ones that we use represent but a small fraction of the total variety of bacteria "out there." It is quite possible that there are more varieties of bacteria on this planet than there are human beings.

Bacteria are the original microbes, a term we give to them and three other types of single-celled organisms, which can only be seen individually through a microscope.[24] We tend to think, with quiz-show simplicity, that everything in the natural world can be categorized as animal, vegetable, or mineral. Yet for most of the time that there has been a planet

Earth, there were just minerals and microbes. Paleontologists have discovered fossil records that indicate the emergence of bacteria during Earth's first billion years. Their various manifestations and single-celled descendants were all the life there was on Earth for the next 2 to 3 billion years. If Earth were 100 years old, then the first bacteria would have arrived by its seventh year, and the first human beings 12 hours ago.

It is microbes that fashioned the atmosphere that supports all plant and animal life, creating the original oxygen through photosynthesis in the oceans. Algae, essentially photosynthetic bacteria, play an important part in managing the planet's delicate atmosphere, undertaking 70 percent of the photosynthesis on Earth and creating vast quantities of oxygen in the process. As a primary food source, they provide the very basis of the huge oceanic food chain.

Although more than three quarters of the air we breathe is nitrogen, plants cannot access this essential food by themselves. Soil based nitrogen-fixing bacteria do it for them. Bacterial friends such as rhizobium live around a plant's roots taking in pure nitrogen and expelling it into the soil as nitrates and nitrites, which the plants can absorb. The pea- and bean-producing legumes provide dedicated chambers in their plant bodies, which serve as free hotels for their helpful bacteria friends to inhabit.

Within our own digestive system, bacteria make up the intestinal flora that line our stomach and gut. They help break down our food into nutrients that our blood is able to absorb and circulate. A healthy gut will be lined with tens of billions of these "bugs." They are the friends who take a beating during a heavy dose of antibiotics, needing to recover before our digestion feels right again. Our skin averages about 100,000 bacteria per square centimeter as part of our own indigenous protective coating. A spoonful of good garden soil could easily contain over a billion bacteria. They are everywhere, they are in abundance and there is no way we could live without them.

Wild microbes floating in the air helped fashion the first leavened loaves of bread—lightened by the gaseous emissions of billions of microbes munching through the dough. It was microbes that made the first alcohols, rotting sugars through fermentation long before humans ever discovered its addictive intoxication. Other microbes turn milk into hundreds of varieties of cheese, yogurt, and other fermented and aged dairy products. Sauerkraut and most pickles rely on controlled rotting by bacteria. Microbes are essential to the manufacture of most traditional soya foods: fermented soya sauce, fermented miso soya paste, the tempeh of Indonesia, and slimy natto of Japan. A surprising amount of our diet relies upon foods that use microbes as an essential part of the cooking process.

Imagine the garbage problem we would have on Earth with no bacteria or fungi to decompose all the organic waste of the planet. Autumn leaves would just pile up year after year and eventually suffocate the forests, or create one hell of a fire hazard. A "bouquet" of maple leaves that I collected in Hyde Park has been hanging from my office ceiling for more than 12 years (as I write). They get a wash and dry every few years to freshen up, but are still as firm as when they first dried out. It is the action of microbes that helps dead leaves decay into soil.

You have probably never ever wondered why termites can digest wood and we cannot. They couldn't without the dedicated microbes in their gut doing the digestion. All the carbon content in dead organisms needs the decomposing action of bacteria to make it available as soil nutrition to future generations of plants. It is the fervent working of microbes that produces the steaming heat at the center of a compost heap, turning old vegetable matter into rich soil. Although individually small, microbes are essential to most processes of life on this planet— including those involving the transition of life materials from one form to another.

Bacteria are able to live in an incredibly wide range of conditions. They can be found in the frozen bleakness of Antarctica and in the heart of a dry parched desert. Recently, when we could build a machine able to withstand the intense conditions, bacteria were found living near deep hot water ocean vents, at temperatures up to 121°Centigrade. They can live on just about anything, including sunlight, water, rock, and metal, as well as just about every organic material on the planet. Some of them seem be able to survive without the light or life-producing products of a local star.

Unlike us, bacteria do not have a basic life cycle starting with birth and ending in death. They start life as a single cell and end life as a pretty identical-looking single cell, with more life experience and perhaps a few tweaks to its genes. There are many things that can kill bacteria but old age is not necessarily among them. Death is not an inevitable fact of life for bacteria although it is something that they sooner or later encounter in this rough-and-tumble world.

One of the many contributors to the success of bacteria is their ability to survive in a dormant state for extended periods—sometimes millions of years. This can help them to deal with the sorts of changes that would wipe out most other life forms on the planet. It would also make it possible for them to travel through space without the need for pressurized outfits and breathing equipment. On Earth, bacteria that were locked in Alaskan permafrost for 32,000 years have been revived, with similar claims made for bacteria found in salt crystals 250 million years old. They are the world's oldest living organisms.

Sex between bacteria is very different from that between animals or that between plants. As far as sex goes (and most other facts of life) we are much closer to turnips than we are to bacteria. Bacteria don't need sex to reproduce; they just double themselves up and then divide into two (binary fission). In ideal conditions, one bacterium could become one billion after just 10 hours.

But single-sex sex, successful though it is, would soon meet a dead end without genetic diversity, so occasionally bacteria will "get it on" with other bacteria. Bacterial sex is called conjugation, and involves one bacterium sticking a thin tube called a pilus into the other one and dropping off a useful segment of its DNA in the process. The DNA recipient will get genes that are likely to enhance its own future survival by enabling it to endure harsher conditions, resist poisons, or ingest new kinds of food. Bacteria are even thought to be capable of selecting useful genes from a dead donor, picking up DNA that is floating in the water. Both the speed and the selective evolution of bacteria help to explain their success rate in overcoming the chemicals and antibiotics we develop to kill them. They are survivors, and have been for a very long time.

We often are impressed by the precision and intelligence of raw nature. Just how is it that something without a perceivable brain is able to recognize desirable genes in the first place and then share them with friends, or grab them and incorporate them into its own genetic makeup? We clever humans only discovered the existence of genes a few generations ago and have only recently begun to unscramble them and understand the significance of particular ones. Bacteria have been doing this intuitively for billions of years—and very successfully. We cannot say the same for the human geneticists who are tampering in ignorance with our biological future as they force together gene combinations impossible in nature.

We have never really understood how it is that in a community of millions of ants each one somehow works in a knowing harmony with the whole. At times, the colony seems more like a single entity than a collection of ants. Is something similar happening within a community or colony of bacteria? Might the combined intelligence of billions of bacteria be adding up to a bigger intelligence?

In 2002, British scientists announced the discovery that a colony of bacteria were caught somehow sending messages to a related colony undergoing drug tests nearby. The communication from outside helped the threatened bacteria to better survive. As you can imagine, the researchers were puzzled by this phenomenon.

Perhaps bacteria, as a life form, should be regarded as an intelligent group entity, rather than as billions of disconnected individuals. They have been evolving for a thousand times as long as us, enjoying a few billion years of life experience compared to our few million. Perhaps they developed a few useful traits and abilities over all those years— things that we have no concept of when it comes to our human experience of intelligence and communication.

It is a sad, though understandable, fact of modern life that the only microbes of which most people seem to be aware are the tiny minority that threaten us—those nasty germs. The consequences of exposure to these can range from mild discomfort to death depending on our state of health plus whether, and how, we deal with the situation. Innumerable other microbes keep the planet going, protect us, nourish us and are invaluable to life itself. Yet people have come to think of microbes, especially bacteria, as dangerous enemies to be avoided and killed at every possible opportunity.

Sales are booming in antibacterial soaps, household products and plastic goods, fueled by a paranoid mentality that seeks to kill everything that could possibly pose a threat. In the process, vast numbers of innocent and often beneficial bacteria are also destroyed—collateral damage in the quest to crush all disease. But good health is not about avoiding all possible contact with unfriendly bacteria and then being overwhelmed every time we do encounter them, or having to fight back with poisons that damage us as well.

Good health is about resisting unwanted invaders in the first place, and having an immune system able to recognize and tackle them if they do appear. Together with other defences, our bodies are well equipped with various single-celled "terminators" that are able to recognize, hunt down, and kill unwanted microbes that get into our system. To do this well, they need training and exercise, particularly in our early years, when the body's natural defense systems are at their fittest. Medical researchers are beginning to discover that growing up in sanitized, bacteria-free environments is contributing to growing levels of allergy and disease among children and adults. In some medical communities they are actually injecting young children with specially prepared extract of soil in order to develop their immune systems.

Let's think again about the hundred thousand bacteria living on a square centimeter of normal healthy skin. It is probable that they are there for a reason, as are the nutrient-processing bacteria in our guts and the oxygen-producing ones in the oceans. A healthy personal bacterial shield might well protect us from the unwanted microbes that create unpleasant odors, skin problems, and infections following scratches and scrapes. Understandably, there are few corporations interested in spending millions of dollars to fund research into areas of science that might not promote sales of their existing array of products.

Bacteria are powerful and little understood organisms, seemingly capable of assuming a higher intelligence founded upon the total numbers living within a colony. We would not be here were it not for their tireless planetary preparations over billions of years, nor could we continue to exist without their presence both inside our bodies and outside in our world, or their world, depending on how one looks at it.

Though smaller than our bodies' cells, there are more bacteria cells living in and on our bodies than there are body cells within those bodies—four or five times as many, in fact. We are dependent on bacteria to the same degree than we are dependent upon air, water, and nourishment. And they will be here long after we have passed from the scene. They will be here until Sun itself expires and some of them might even endure beyond that.

Water

inanimate, active, and alive

WATER IS VITAL to organic life on this planet, and the major element making Earth unique among the planets. It is such a special feature that scientists and the public are always excited by evidence pointing to it on other planets or moons of this solar system. The glass of water we drink today has been recycling itself for billions of years—it could once have been part of the body of a brontosaurus or even have arrived on a comet. Water is an essential component of all forms of animal and plant life on the planet, making up some two-thirds of our own body weight.

Over two-thirds of the planet is covered by liquid water. It pervades the atmosphere as vapor, manifesting in the skies as clouds, rain, ice, and snow. "Dry" land is permeated by water, running free in rivers or sitting quietly in large repositories, above and below ground. Landscaped layers of solid water cover both the icy reaches of the north and south poles. Water is the only substance on the planet that exists naturally as solid, liquid and gas. It is very special, which is why it has for long been invested with spirit, and was accorded great respect and importance by early cultures.

Oceans are not simply vast repositories of water, waiting to be evaporated into vapour that will feed the world's weather systems. They are complex, organized and well-regulated entities—each of the world's major oceans possessing different characteristics from the others, different personalities. In each of the planet's oceans we find massive currents—clearly defined rivers transporting billions of tons of water across hemispheres, without resort to any unnatural power source or pipes for containment.

At the peak of its flow the North Atlantic Current (Gulf Stream) carries 750 times the volume of water that empties from the mouth of the mighty Amazon River. This brings warmth to Europe. The major Humboldt Current rises from the Antarctic to sweep along the western coastline of South America. The fish-rich shores of Japan depend upon nutrients delivered by the 100-kilometer-wide Kuroshio ("black salt") Current. There are many more ocean currents, some of them running deep below the surface. Little is known of the purpose of these currents although their effect upon ocean ecology and the world's climate is immense.

The average depth of the ocean bottom is four to five times as great as the average height of dry land, which makes up just 25 percent of the planet's surface. There is roughly 10 to 20 times more land surface beneath the waves than above them, providing vast habitats for an array of creatures even more incredible than those existing on land. We tend to look upon oceans as sources of seafood and a means to transport things cheaply in ships and tankers. Yet their vast expanses contain 97 percent of this planet's water, providing a home to the vast majority of its inhabitants.

Irrigation of the land with seawater desalinated by fusion power is ancient. It's called "rain."
—MICHAEL MCCLARY

For countless millions of years water has been rising skywards from the land and the sea, later to be distributed by the planet's atmosphere. When rain falls on dry land it does not just roll downhill into rivers and end up in one ocean or another, to evaporate and come down again as rain—which is what one might expect it to do. Beneath the quarter of our planet covered in land lies a vast underground system of waterworks containing over 30 times as much water as is found in all the planet's lakes, inland seas, and rivers put together. Most of the water falling to land travels underground under the influence of gravity, penetrating every nook and cranny and crevice, filling the holes of any porous rock. Eventually, water reaches a layer of solid rock or clay and can sink no more. Now it takes form and moves in slow currents through the underground landscape, self-organizing into all manner of activity, creating everything from aquifers to mountain springs, underground rivers, hot springs, and geysers.

While rivers and lakes will be swelled and fed by the rains, the primary source and sustenance of those rivers and lakes arises from underground stores of water, coming up as springs, or fed through subterranean channels. A torrential rainfall may rip through a mountain valley as a flash flood travelling at 50 mph, and thousands of years later gush forth from a rock wall halfway up the same mountain, feeding into the stream that will later grow to become a mighty river.

Without human interference, rivers seldom choose the shortest and more efficient straight path to the sea, but prefer to snake along like an uncoiling spiral, tapping into some universal energy pattern and distributing their nourishment over a larger area. Like an architect with art at heart, the relentless downward flow, over thousands and millions of years, carves valleys of all shapes into the environment, finding its route around everything.

In a natural unmanaged river, currents arise within the waters that keep the banks orderly and prevent silt from building up and forming blockages. It seems almost to be grooming itself. The life of a river ebbs and flows, swollen in springtime by the melting snows and shrunken by droughts and long dry summers. Over the grander geological time scale, the river will shape its entire surrounding environment, whilst sustaining and affecting its personal ecosystem of plants and animals. Many streams are protected from evaporation by the canopy of trees that they encourage to grow along their banks—synergy between the animate and the inanimate. Despite the major impact that rivers have upon the landscape and the life living upon land, they hold barely a millionth of the planet's water.

Much of the water falling on land will return to the atmosphere without travelling through rivers to the ocean. It will be evaporated straight from the ground, or be released by trees and plants in the breathing process known as transpiration.

Earth's atmosphere holds some ten times as much water as its rivers, though the maximum concentration that it can carry is 4 percent of its volume. When this level is reached, it is termed 100 percent humidity and the shops sell out of air conditioners. The atmospheric moisture can be invisibly distributed as clear vapor, or organized into one or another of several different species of clouds.[25] Each of these has different shapes, characteristics, and behavior. A common fluffy cumulus cloud may contain many hundreds of tons of water, though averaging just half a gram of it per cubic meter.

Some clouds have distinct borders, some are fuzzy, and many clouds will assemble to live in "communities" of thousands, when it can be difficult to distinguish where one cloud begins and another ends. Enough cumulus clouds can, on occasion, organize themselves into giant swirling hurricanes, sucking moisture from the sea and wreaking devastation upon island and coastal communities. We will often find more than one type of cloud variety in the same sky, but they will usually have their different cruising altitudes. Most clouds are ephemeral creatures, continually forming and dissolving in the sky. Turn your head away for a few minutes and when you look back there can be an entirely new skyscape.

The large cumulonimbus thunderclouds with the anvil-shaped top are more solitary creatures, though they often will roam in a loosely grouped pack. They live longer than most clouds, occasionally existing for a day or more and travelling long distances. They are able to carry 10 to 20 times as much water per cubic meter as a common cumulus. One of these thunderclouds can be massive enough to darken the whole of a big town or large sections of a city, while all might be Sunshine and peace outside of its coverage. Beneath it the land will be receiving torrents of rain and bolts of thunderous lightning, all emanating from the dynamic processes taking place within the waters of the thundercloud.

Scientists understand the process that goes on within clouds and can explain how it all works—in the same way they can explain how our breathing and blood oxygenation works. There is a lot of process going on in that cloud—much more than we find in a single drop of water. Is it all just natural events and processes that are randomly combining to assemble this relatively complex entity? Or are the assembled trillions of water molecules somehow emanating an intelligence that is involved in the maintenance and function of the cloud? It was very common for our ancestors to recognize spirit entities and even gods representing thunder.

It is clouds that redistribute water around the globe, transporting it from the oceans and the land, to release it hundreds or thousands of miles later. They feed the world's enormous underground storage capacity giving life to its flowing rivers and filling its lakes while wetting the land and feeding the life upon it. Clouds are just one of the amazing incarnations water can take during its existence on the planet. They seem like the rapid-reaction force of the planet's atmosphere, part of its essential maintenance system.

Over 75 percent of the world's fresh water is locked up in ice, most of that located at the planet's two poles. We can but guess at the relevance of these icy caps to a planet thought to have a fiercely hot molten center. It is above these frozen open icescapes that the molecules of Earth's atmosphere are able to mix directly with the charged particles of the solar wind, giving rise to the dancing lights of the aurora borealis. Perhaps some form of information exchange could be taking place here, with the giant ice sheets of frozen water performing like intelligent planetary receptors. One must wonder what effect the eventual melting of the Arctic icecap will have upon these northern lights.

Yet more fresh water is locked into the planet's glaciers—massive rivers of solid ice, slowly and inexorably moving across the landscape, cutting through and reshaping everything in their path. Not that long ago, much of Europe and North America was covered in these giant rivers of ice and some suggest that the whole of Homo sapiens' history has taken place within a temporary lull in an ongoing ice age.

Starting from just a tiny crystal, water is able to form the incredible snowflake—each one unique, though like clouds, there are identified varieties. From its birth as a few frozen molecules of water, each crystal creation is thereafter fashioned by the many thousands of responses that it makes to every micro-twist of temperature, air pressure, humidity and wind direction encountered on its drifting path to the planet's surface. When Johannes Kepler published his treatise "On the Six-Cornered Snowflake" in 1611 he found it necessary to consider that "each and any starlet of snow" might have the "individual soul" that he perceived as the "animating principle" in plants. He dismissed it as absurd, however, thinking this was going a little too far. Each detail of the snow crystal's design, however, reflects a memory of its own unique existence.

KENNETH LIBBRECHT

Which brings us to another remarkable property of water—memory. This is manifested in different ways. On a most simple level, when we are flying from coastal airports and across seas, it is often possible to see the wake of a ship for many hours after the vessel has vanished beyond the horizon. One would think that the swell and the wave and

)f the ocean's surface would soon remove all trace of a
t the memory remains for a long time. Polynesian sail-
discover islands that were many hundreds of miles dis-
:ing and tracking the altered patterns in the waves that
washed by their boats.

Water also seems able to capture and remember the vibration of physical substances with which is has been in contact—even when the original substance is no longer present. It is this property that makes it possible to transfer the vibration of remedies to homeopathic medicines, even from poisonous substances. This property of water is also credited with generating rage, disbelief, and scorn from scientists and rational thinkers. It defies their logic system and therefore cannot work, whatever the experience of people who use and work with it.

It is thought that the unique dipolar hydrogen bonds in water molecules enable them to create a latticework structure capable of reproducing and remembering the structure of atoms and molecules with which the water has been in contact. This could be the "rational" explanation for water retaining the effects of a substance when no molecules of that substance remain in the water. But there could be some other explanation, one that is consistent with this property of memory being transferred to homeopathic tablets when the water is removed.

This property of memory was demonstrated in 1984 by one of France's top allergy specialists, Professor Jacques Benveniste. His laboratory was testing white blood cells for their reaction to certain allergens, when one of his best lab technicians reported a strange result. Before testing an allergen, it had been accidentally diluted well beyond the usual point, leaving just a few molecules remaining in the solution. The error was discovered after the technician had recorded a reaction from the exposed white blood cells. The results were checked and re-checked and kept coming up, even at higher dilutions. Benveniste's results were published, seeming to give credit to the claims of homeopathy. Similar results were produced by at least five other respected research establishments before, in 1988, the scientific establishment organized a vigorous discrediting of the findings' validity. The highly respected Benveniste subsequently lost his funding, his facilities, and his reputation.

In 2003, the Swiss chemist Louis Rey used thermo-luminescence to view the altered structure of hydrogen bonds in water with a common salt solution. Out of curiosity he performed homeopathic dilutions on his original water until there could be no molecules of salt remaining, and was surprised to find that the hydrogen bonds retained the pattern of the salt molecules. The controversy returned to a scientific community still reluctant to accept such notions.

Many believe in the concept of holy water that retains the vibrations given to it by a spiritual person, and in the ability of special springs to produce water possessing beneficial qualities. Perhaps it is not simply a matter of people's faith, or the mineral content of particular waters that gives them their properties. In 2001 Japanese researcher, Masaru Emoto published his first book, *Messages from Water,* showing photographs of water crystals using a technique that he spent several years creating. In the photos, it appears as though the water is physically responding to events around it, forming ugly and messy crystals when exposed to negative thoughts or words, and beautifully structured ones when exposed to positive thoughts or words. The implications of this, for all of us, are quite thought provoking when we consider the amount of water that is in us, in most of the food we eat, in nearly all the growing things on the planet and in the oceans covering most of the planet's surface.

Few scientists have ever studied water as a living entity and sought to understand the phenomena that go along with that. Victor Schauberger (1885-1958) was the exception. He investigated the properties of water which no scientist would look at, certainly not one trained to view it as dead matter. He demonstrated how natural rivers use turbulence to keep themselves clean and flowing smoothly. He developed ways to manage and tap the physical and mystical powers of water, determining the temperature at which maximum buoyancy was achieved. He understood the inextricable linkage of forests and trees—how trees bring water into the soil, later releasing it through natural springs. He correctly predicted how the depletion of forest would dangerously affect the vitality of rivers and lakes worldwide.

Victor Schauberger understood water like no other. Look him up on the Internet or get his enlightening book, *Living Water.* You could say that he understood water like Nicola Tesla understood electricity. But he is less well known, and even fewer of his remarkable discoveries have survived to benefit mankind. Herr Schauberger would have been delighted, though not surprised, by the work of Masuru Emoto.

Water is, one could say, part of the essential vegetable trinity. With carbon dioxide and the energy of Sun, water gives life to seeds, and structure to all vegetable life, from the humble algae to the towering redwood tree. It truly is the stuff of life. Is it so difficult to imagine that this stuff of life might have the capacity to experience life itself, playing a part in its own well-organized and purposeful existence?

Fire and flame
consuming force, transforming gift

ALTHOUGH IT SEEMS like such an essential commodity today, it is not so difficult to imagine a world before electricity came onto the scene. This was a world illuminated only by the light of living flame, heated by a fire or a furnace, and propelled by foot, animal-power and more recently the fire-powered internal combustion engine (cars). Without electricity, we developed fine cuisines using fire to steam, boil, bake, or grill our foods in pots and pans that were cleverly fashioned, by fire, from clay or metal and glass. We were able to live in a recognizable world of heated houses, with fine furniture and fabrics, high cultures, empires, wars, sports, and the like.

But can we ever comprehend what it would have been like before we learned how to manage fire? Imagine knowing fire only as an uncontrollable and frightening phenomenon, most likely to be witnessed following a lightning strike unless you happened to live near an active volcano. These were truly the dark ages of our species. Anthropologists may one day discover just when we became the first animal to huddle around a fire, rather than run for our life away from it.

The Greeks credit the demi-god Prometheus with taking the secret of fire from the gods, and sharing it with us. For this he was severely punished by Zeus. Anthropologists have found evidence that fire may have been in use by humans up to a million years ago. However it is that we learned to manage and use fire, this skill probably did more to define us as human beings than any other landmark in the history of our species. Our world has never been the same since.

Imagine now, if you can, an existence without any flame to illuminate the darkness of night—with only the skins of hairier animals and huddling together to provide us with warmth in cold weather. We probably even needed fire to make the transition to "cave-man" since most caves are tricky to navigate at night, or very deeply by day unless you are equipped with built-in radar. It might well have been more comfortable sleeping in some kind of tree house than wandering around in the scary darkness of a cave with who knows what for company.

For thousands of years, with weak bodies and no tools, we were more likely to be the prey than the predator, and may have eaten a more vegetarian diet, as do most apes. Food was not only all raw, but all those foods which require cooking to become safe, edible or digestible were unavailable to us. Fire completely transformed our diet, our environment, and our culture. We would have possessed fire for much of the Stone Age, before discovering how to melt metals strong enough to make lasting tools, weapons and objects of beauty.

To a human being who had never known fire as a friend, the technology of a candle that burned steadily and gave off light would have seemed quite miraculous. It would almost be like having your own miniature Sun on tap. The analogy may sound extreme, but it is not so far-fetched. Both share the function of steadily releasing an even stream of heat and photons over an extended period of time. Both are fire elements, the candle releasing fire power from Sun that was laid down eons ago. And though our star's fuel reserves will last far longer than that of any candle, just how many other phenomenon are there in the natural Universe that share this steady photon-producing function?

There is another aspect to this Sun and candle analogy, which came to me while spending a night in the garden with a candle during the early stages of work on this book. After some time, I got a sense of the candle flame as being a conscious little fire entity—something alive that was sharing my space. When a light breeze came, it appeared to be struggling for its life and then coming back from near extinction time and time again. Have you ever watched how a candle in the wind fights to survive? You may well think that I was on some psychedelic drug at the time, but if you ask any fireman he will tell you just how convincingly a fire behaves like a living being once it has taken hold of a building or a forest.

Though it has no form or material substance, flame is a manifestation of the basic power behind Universe—lying, as it does, at the borderland between the visible world of matter and the invisible world of energy.

Many tens of millions of candles are lit every day by followers of different religions—playing their part as the conduits carrying our thoughts, prayers and energies to destinations unknown to the Royal Mail or FedEx. We find the candle, this mini-Sun, to be as universal to religions of the world as is the Golden Rule. From time immemorial we have used candles to help carry wishes and messages to non-visible dimensions. Technology may never be able to develop a light bulb able to display the same connective capacity.

Fire plays an important part in the worship of Zoroastrians, who have traditionally maintained many sacred fires set within dedicated temples. Two fires are still maintained which have been burning steadily since well before the time of Christ. In times of upheaval, the sacred fires might be hidden for years in secret caves. Because of the reverence with which it was held, no waste or rubbish was ever added to a fire. Fire was considered to pervade the other creations of the primary gOd Ahura Mazda. Zoroastrians considered fire to be the controller of Sun, and therefore the regulator of the seasons and other aspects of life on Earth.

The inner fire is the most important thing mankind possesses.
—EDITH SODERGRAN

What is happening when flame produces light? Science is not very revealing on this, although it is clear that light seems to arise whenever electrons get excited. They do this as they jump from higher to lower energy orbits around their nuclei. Whenever you see light, there are excited electrons behind it. In the heart of Sun they are creating light as a by-product of the atomic transmutation of hydrogen to helium. In a wood fire they are excited by the heat and the dissolution of the structure originally formed through the light of photosynthesis. In a candle they are a by-product of the hot conversion of hard wax into gas and glowing atoms of carbon.

Some bacteria long ago figured out how to excite electrons and make light, and are occasionally harnessed by deep-sea creatures and insects for illumination. In the light bulb it is the highly excitable electrons of the tungsten filament that emit light as the current travels through them. But just how and why an excited electron releases a newborn photon may forever be a mystery.

We may manage and direct fire in our lives with great skills, but can easily forget that even the humble smolder of a cigarette can turn into a flame capable of engulfing an entire house or forest in its thus-extended lifespan. A hot enough fire will destroy any matter known to mankind—all will be reduced to its bare atomic structure in the ferocity of a star's heat. Perhaps the destruction of matter by fire is accompanied by the liberation of spirit, as when a tree is reduced to ashes and gases—released from the confines of matter and geography. Perhaps all spirit ultimately returns to the crucible of fire at the center of Sun, or another star.

A roaring fire commands our fascination—as does a child at play, or a soaring eagle. What is it that we find compelling about flame and fire? Like the light it produces, the secrets of fire may always remain a mystery to us. There is nothing else remotely like it, and for thousands of years we have been finding new applications for it. Today we find increasing applications for fire's by-product, light—and for the electrons that seem to act as the fire element's representative in the material world of atoms. It is fire that gave us the power to develop the culture that so uniquely defines us as human beings. And it is our use and abuse of fire that has the power to ultimately destroy us.

Transmute to live
the food of life

Y OU STARTED LIFE on this planet when two single cells were joined together in a miniature big bang as sperm and egg combined to become one cell. When that new entity first divided into two new cells the building of you began. The major part of your biological development and growth took place as these two cells became a baby over the next nine months.

Before a digestive system developed you took nourishment straight from your mother's blood. But ever since leaving the womb, virtually all of your development, growth, and energy along the way has been sourced and fuelled by the food taken in through your mouth.

It is food which has provided the building materials for your body in the first place, and which continues to repair and replace the cells from which it is built. It is food which converts into the energy that powers your heart beat, sustaining work and dance while it fuels the bioelectrical exchanges going on between the neurons firing in your brain. Virtually every food we consume, with the exception of salt and some food additives is a form of stored Sunlight. This is originally laid down as energy through the photosynthesis of plants, and subsequently released as energy to sustain the life of those eating the plants, and those eating those eating the plants, and so on up the food chain.

You are an amazing transmutation machine. You can take in carrots, candy bars, baked beans, bread, plums, porridge, hamburgers, or herrings—and turn them into living energy and whatever body parts you need. A carrot takes light, air, water, and earth, converting them into a crunchy, pointy, orange vegetable, and you turn this carrot into a moving, intelligent, seeing, human being. What an amazing world!

Wine is sunlight, held together by water.
—GALILEO

Every time that you eat you are converting some other manifestation of life energy into your own. Eating is the only thing that human beings, and every other animal on the planet, must actually do in order to survive. We cannot stop our heartbeat or our breathing but we can choose to stop eating and die, as many protest-fasters have demonstrated. With the possible exception of communication, there is probably no more commonly shared activity of our species than eating. Like communication, it is also an activity over which we have a great deal of control and opportunity for personal choice.

If there is one essential point to be gained from reading this chapter it is the significance of the fact that your energy is provided by food, your body is built and maintained by it, and your being is powered by it. We frequently hear of people whose paranoia or other psychologically disturbed activity was completely eliminated by removing certain foods from the diet. We often read about severely disturbed children who become normal when their diets are improved. But we are all of us affected all the time by what we eat in far greater ways than generally recognized. What we eat has a great deal to do with our emotions and feelings, our response to situations, and what new situations those responses lead us to. The knowledge of this alone should prompt us to look differently at that which is about to transmute into ourselves.

There are a staggering number of edible vegetable combinations of light, air, water, and earth that are growing on this planet. The same base

ingredients that produce a carrot can also make a grain of rice or a hot
ginger root. The widely different vibrations and life-energies in food are
real, and become you if they have not been processed out by the time
it reaches your plate. Good food enables and even guides you to live
your life much better on many levels—beyond improving simply physical health. But what is good food? The answer cannot fit within these
pages, and ultimately only conscious consuming will enable you to really understand the answer, but here are a few broad tips from my own
life-experience in the field.

Eating, whether done by anteaters, bees, cattle, or human beings, is
essentially the transmutation of one life form's components into another
life form. Just what we consume constitutes a key factor in the success
of our existence upon the planet supplying all that we eat. The simplest
global guidance I ever received on this matter came from George Ohsawa, the father of macrobiotics, who advises us to eat "as far away from
yourself as possible." The closest thing to ourselves that we could eat
is another human being, and most of us find cannibalism instinctively
repulsive. And of course, the closest humans to us are our own family,
which few would eat even if facing starvation on a mountain pass.

The next step away from cannibalism is the eating of fellow mammals like pigs, cattle, horses, sheep, dogs, or cats. Many of us are easily able to make bonding personal relationships and feel close to those
mammals we choose to be our domestic pets. Most dog owners will
willingly spend more on a veterinary operation than it would cost to
replace their dog with a new one.

We share 95 percent or more of our DNA with most domesticated
animals, from pigs to cattle to hamsters to cats. Together with DNA,
the mammals all share recognizable behavioral traits when it comes to
things like territory, fear, sex, parenting, eating, and social interaction.
Many of the hormones, secretions, and fluids of domesticated mammals are similar to our own and capable of affecting human behavior.
Indeed, we harvest animal hormones for this purpose medicinally, taking insulin from pigs to treat diabetes, and HRT products from horse
urine to treat menopausal women. The body chemicals produced by
other mammals during the shock and horror of impending slaughter

are likely to be triggering similar chemical receptors in our own brains, prompting fear, despair, and hostility.

A step further away from our mammalian relatives takes us to birds such as chicken, ducks, or turkeys. Although we can make friends with parrots and canaries and recognize some of our own behavioral traits in bird life, they are much farther away from us than pigs, and share less DNA. We do not eat many reptiles in the West, but my guess is that in this scale they would fall directly before or after birds.

Farther away than birds we come to fish, quite different from us and without lungs or penetrative sex. There are cases of human friendships with some fish (koi carp and large sea-fish) but it is difficult to imagine anyone ever having bonded with an individual herring, sardine, or mackerel. Fish are animals, and in most non-insect-eating cultures they are the animal food farthest from humans. They are relatively blood-free and Muslims and Jews do not need special butchers for fish, though are restricted to eating only seafood with scales on it (no eels or oysters). Many of those who refer to themselves as vegetarian will partake of fish and shellfish from time to time, seeing this type of food to be in a distinctly different category to the meat of ocean mammals or land animals.

The next level of food is made from by-products of animals, such as milk, cheese, butter, yogurt, and eggs. These come somewhere between animals and vegetables and their quality varies enormously depending upon the quality of life of the animals from which they originate. In much of India, the cows that supply milk and dairy products roam freely and are not ground into hamburgers when their milk output drops below a determined level. But then again, I have seen them eating newspapers and greasy cardboard as well as growing green things.

The next step away from ourselves is a huge one, taking us to the vegetable world where the level of DNA sharing begins to drop significantly, and shared characteristics are harder to spot. Even though we still share about half of its DNA, it gets very difficult to empathize with a cabbage, or feel sorry for it when torn from the ground before producing seeds for the next generation. More of us are able to empathize with the plight of a thousand-year-old tree about to be terminated to make tabletops or way for a road. Gardeners love many of their plants and we are told that the plants respond to that love and to communication. But few of us give much thought to killing small vegetables, or would experience compassion as we are cooking them.

Of course, most vegetable food need not even be killed for us to enjoy it. The most prevalent staple foods of our species are those that are gifted to us by the plant world—veritable fruits of the earth. Across the world, seeds have formed much of the basis of our diet for millennia. These incorporate all of our cereals such as rice, wheat, rye, barley, corn, oats, and millet; all of our legumes from soya and kidney beans to lentils and fresh garden peas; all of our oil-bearing seeds such as olives, sesame, peanut, and sunflower; nuts such as almonds, chestnut, and pistachio; seed-bearing fleshy fruits such as apples and apricots, blackberries and pomegranates; seed vegetables such as pumpkins, cucumbers, and marrow; and all those seed-based spices from pepper to cumin to nutmeg. Even to those able to feel sorry for a cabbage, it is bordering on the impossible to empathize with a grain of rice, an almond or an apple— foods which have not had to give up their lives in order for us to consume them.

For a majority of the world population, these fruits of nature are the core staple foods of the diet: carbohydrate-rich cereals, protein-rich legumes, and fat-rich oil seeds. Fresh vegetables, fruit, and animal foods are usually but additions to these core dietary staples. It seems almost obvious that these fruits of nature would be the perfect staple foods of our species. Each of them contains the concentrated nutritional base required to supply a healthy start to the germ of life that they carry.

In "advanced" Western cultures, many have lost any sense or awareness of their diet as being that which fuels and enables this survival in the flesh. Most consumers only understand diet as something to be done to correct something that is wrong—like being overweight or clogged with cholesterol. Sadly, there is often more focus upon what foods are being excluded than upon the more vital question of what is being included in the diet. When not dieting a majority of consumers simply eat what they are accustomed to, selecting that which is easily available and seductively promoted. Little consideration is given to physical health or spiritual well-being. Happily, the minority who think about how they fuel their precious bodies is a fast-growing one.

Though sugar is essential to life, it is refined sugars that have become central to the modern Western diet. Our bodies are designed to slowly convert complex carbohydrate from our food into a steady supply of sugar to our bloodstream. When we feed our body refined sugars instead of complex starchy carbohydrates it is like throwing gasoline on a fire, instead of feeding it with a slow-burning log. Cereal foods such as bread, pasta, rice, barley, oats, corn, and the other grains provide good, steadily released carbohydrate energy and some protein.

Legumes also contribute to carbohydrate energy while providing more protein, which joins with that in cereals to provide building materials as complete as any animal source can provide. People who eat refined sugar feel the need for it every day and in virtually every meal, whether consumed in ketchup, breakfast cereals, jams, soups, pastries, candy, and soft drinks, or added by the spoonful. Simple sugars will one day be recognized as more addictive than most illegal drugs—and far more destructive to our health and emotional stability than many of them.

Our miraculous bodies are able to take in an enormous variety of foods and transmute them into living human beings. The choice of what we want to be is ours. The spirit in which this transmutation is undertaken has a bearing upon what type of energy and life we receive from it. A plateful of fish and chips, enjoyed in good company with great relish and appreciation, can provide better nourishment than a meal of organic rice, beans, and salad that is consumed in the course of a stressful argument.

Another outlook on enjoyment came to me one day as I was about to tuck into a sardine sandwich at my kitchen table. Those little sardines had probably swum around for a few months dodging marauding tuna, dolphins, and sea birds—all the time grazing here and there on food that had itself spent days or weeks of living growth, before meeting its sardine. The wheat plant had spent a whole season soaking up sunlight and air and water to give us its seeds for flour. Then time and effort were expended to turn it into bread, involving billions of yeast munching away and belching out carbon dioxide to fluff it up. The lettuce spent a month or more getting crisp and juicy and I had spent five minutes putting it all together with some mustard and homemade mayonnaise. As I reached for a magazine to read while eating, I suddenly thought "hell no!" The least I can do is be with this sandwich while eating it—tasting and experiencing and positively enjoying it as all this accumulated life commences the process of becoming me.

To be healthy in this world it should ideally not be necessary to know anything about proteins, carbohydrates, and fats. When we tread this path we run the risk of become increasingly reductionist and thinking that we need to know all about vitamins and specific amino acids and minerals and trace elements of everything we consume—be sure and take a reference book to dinner. This attitude can sometimes take us further away from understanding the nature of food, rather than closer. Mankind only discovered vitamins and nutritional science as a result of the diseases that followed on the heels of the introduction of processed, unbalanced and denatured foods to civilized diets. Look at your food, taste it, feel it, and feel for it. Is it real? Do you want it to become you?

My initial and more important overall guidance and knowledge came from the originator of the macrobiotic diet, George Ohsawa, who had an enormous influence upon the format of the world's now substantial natural food industry. The macrobiotic food companies of the 1970s were the first to ever sell, to the natives of the United States or Europe, a host of now standard products. These included such items as brown rice and most whole cereals, chickpeas and most beans and legumes, sesame seeds, sunflower seeds, rice cakes, tahini, tofu, miso, shoyu, ginseng, seaweeds, and much more. They were also the first companies to actively develop and distribute organic food products.

Though he gave much good advice about food and diet, Ohsawa always maintained that a person with true health could eat anything they liked and transmute it into a happy, healthy human being. Of course, the wants and desires of this healthy person are shaped and affected by their understanding of food and its effect upon them. In my own experience, once I have noticed the cause-effect connection between, for example, aching joints and the recent consumption of tomatoes, the problem begins to resolve itself. After going through the aches a few times and recognizing what is prompting them, I lose those urges that would need suppressing. Tomatoes become less attractive to me, though they do not become taboo. One of the appeals of macrobiotics to me is that it is a diet of *what I do eat* and not a diet based upon what I do not eat.

You might need to read Ohsawa to understand just what he means by "true health", which goes well beyond lack of disease to incorporate concepts such as joy, lack of arrogance, freedom, gratitude, and more. His definition of food incorporates what we take in through the eyes and the ears—the food of our minds and our senses too. And he recommended in the mid '60s that we eat locally produced food for our better health, long before any concept of food-miles or carbon footprints came into being.

Many are the sages and teachers who can lead us towards better performance and fulfilment in various aspects of our lives. That is not the remit of this book and I have strayed—albeit into an area that was for many years the primary business of my life, and which is still of great importance to me.

When seeking the sort of information that will make you happier, healthier, and more fulfilled in your life, avoid those who want to give you lists of rules. Look for teachers who, within their field, can give you the tools to understand and know what choices to make, and what routes to take—yourself. Life will always throw new and unexpected information and situations upon us. Learn from them, and develop an intuition that you can trust. At some point you will have to make decisions when neither good advice nor books are to hand. Be ready.

Luck favors the well prepared.

—AN OLD ADAGE

Beauty and the beholder
do flowers know it?

L ET US TAKE to task that time-honored phrase "beauty is in the eye of the beholder." Though it undoubtedly has a nice ring to it, does it really hold true? Are we not usually shaking our heads with disbelief when we use this cliché, trying to figure how on earth person X could find any beauty in object Y or person Z? It can be useful as a politically correct way of expressing disagreement.

There will always be those who find some things beautiful that others find mundane or repellent. Arguing over beauty and art is stimulating, making us look at thing in new ways. But it is fair to say that Quasimodo would not get as many hits at the dating agency as would Robert Redford. Neither will the art of Adolf Hitler ever rank with that of Van Gogh, as he, like many other aspiring artists, once fondly hoped. Has anybody ever looked up at a clear starry night or a glorious sunset and thought them ugly? There are few who hate the sight of flowers.

We often consider ourselves to be uniquely able to appreciate beautiful things in the world. One does not often notice a cow or a sparrow pausing to appreciate the setting Sun or suspect they could ever be moved enough to gasp at the beauty of Van Gogh's sunflowers. The human race is assumed to be the only species that has the spare time and the natural inclination to do such things, and may well be unique in its ability to appreciate the beauty of the cosmos.

Anything without sense organs as we know them—eyes, ears, taste, touch—is assumed to have no sense awareness or sensory appreciation. Plants, presumed to lack all of these senses except perhaps touch, are generally thought to be unaware of either their surroundings or their own being. Even though a sunflower twists its head always towards Sun, we never think that somehow that sunflower could actually be enjoying the beauty of Sunlight, even though its every gene seems to be designed for this purpose.

Beauty is a form of genius—is higher, indeed, than genius, as it needs no explanation. It is of the great facts in the world like sunlight, or springtime, or the reflection in dark water of that silver shell we call the moon.
—OSCAR WILDE

How are we to know what means and methods the plant world has of keeping in touch with its surroundings? Most plants visibly react to all manner of external stimuli, knowing when Sun comes up and when seasons change. Some believe that certain plants are even able to anticipate the severity or mildness of the approaching seasonal change. We may not know how they do it all, but plants are well equipped to know what they need to know to get on with their lives. It is quite possible that they are enjoying sensory facilities that we do not have, facilities that we cannot even imagine.

Botanists generally assume that plants have no sense of beauty. They will stretch Darwinian principles to the very edge to try and explain how any given flower, in the wild, has evolved into its particular colors and shapes as a chance evolutionary progression. How can we possibly believe that flowers, or the plants that produce them, have no sense of their own beauty? Is it not a bit arrogant to assume that these flowers create such elegance and beauty with no intent, no appreciation, no vanity and nothing but genetic efficiency in mind? Are we the only thing there is that appreciates the beauty of a delicate orchid deep in the rainforest, or the iridescent colors of a butterfly?

When cats first smell the scent of something like smoked mackerel, do they find it to be a beautiful smell, as well as a pointer to food? When a peahen is surveying the plume of the peacock, is she as capable of appreciating its beauty, as are we? When birds announce the approaching Sun with a chorus of song, might some appreciation of the beauty of life be involved?

Even though we may not know how other life forms appreciate beauty, we cannot assume that life's most beautiful creations are only appreciated by our fine senses. Beauty is likely to be prompting pleasure, whether humans are there to behold it or not.

Beauty is not in the face;
beauty is a light in the heart.
—KAHLIL GIBRAN

Que sera, sera
what to do with a house guest like us?

P ERHAPS IT WAS not accidental that the occasion of the last well-documented "end of the world" (our world, at least) was caused by years of darkness, rain, and the big flood. Over a hundred different cultural histories around the world refer to a historical restart for humanity after floods covered the land. Many of these legends refer to a Noah-type character who received advance notifications, thereby enabling him to save a selection of species as seed for another beginning.

Might a conscious Sun or Earth, wanting a new start on the planet for whatever reason, have somehow initiated the historical Flood? The Earth and its myriad components appear to operate as a combined organism, producing features such as its weather systems. The greatest outside influence on such weather systems comes from the Sun. If there is some consciousness at play in these bodies then it might have the power to affect their effect upon the weather.

This time round we are faced with a major crisis as global warming inexorably heats the planet, raising its waters from below. We finally begin to recognize that much of the threat we face arises from the environment's response to our own insensitive behavior. It's that old feedback loop again. Much of this clearly has been our own doing: spraying millions of tons of CFCs into the air; dispersing some 75,000 other chemicals into the environment; burning down forests for short-term gain;

poisoning our land to provide food for billions of farm animals whose combined farts add more to the greenhouse effect than all forms of transport combined; slowly poisoning ourselves in the consumption of these animals. Somebody must be laughing at the irony and the sheer stupidity of it all.

It is primarily our "dumb sun" mindset which leads us to believe that there can only be mechanical aspects at play, such as those cited above, in this complex and climactic shift of climate. Perhaps our near universal ingratitude to Sun, our light-bulb-in-the-sky attitude to this miraculous giver of life, could be an underlying factor of the unsettling climate change that we are facing. Then again, perhaps it is arrogant to even suggest that Sun would bother to get so involved.

The other causative factor, on a sphere with a joined-up Gaia consciousness, could be the planet's response to the daily insults we throw at an Earth also viewed, for practical purposes, as inanimate—an Earth that according to science is an unlikely, though fortunate, accident of the cosmos. An Earth which, according to the three Abrahamic religions, is a raw materials cupboard put here specifically for us by gOd. Global warming is not the only problem we face, as extreme geological activity increases, water tables drop, oceans rise, oil runs out, topsoil disappears, and human vitality declines.

Suppose, for a moment, that we are a special creation, tuned more to gOd than others, and more able to wonder upon and appreciate the joys of being alive in this beautiful world. Though the supporting evidence for this assumption is ever diminishing, it still holds validity. We then elevate this specialness to the point where we see nothing else as having a valid claim to existence—other than to benefit our own. We develop an undefined and intellectual gOd to worship and give rarely a second thought to the Sun or our planet Earth—clearly the twin facilitators of all life on this globe. Our prevailing mindset does not even view other animals as valid harbors of consciousness, let alone any of gOd's creations lacking a stomach and central nervous system. And then we are puzzled as to why we experience so many difficulties fitting our human civilization into this harmonically integrated organism. Planet Earth is happy to share many of its treasures and facilities with us, possibly its most intelligent ever guests. But it is, sadly, true that we have come to ravage and savage our beautiful host planet with little, if any, thought or respect to its own being-ness. Just what kind of a houseguest are we?

Science will be primarily looking for traceable cause and effect reactions in order to explain the ozone hole, rising sea levels, increasing seismic activity and so forth. But we cannot ignore the possibility that a conscious Sun and a conscious Earth are themselves subtly modulating the changes in such a way as to respond correctively to our human assault upon the planet.

A conscious and divine Sun, looking at this planet, might be disappointed at the obstacles that our gifted species has placed in the way of enjoying the gift of life on Earth. It might despair at the sheer destruction we wreak upon each other, and our thoughtless damage to the planet. There could even be such disappointment that another new start is called for. It is a shame for all concerned, but what's a few hundred thousand years to put together a new garden on Earth? Compared to an 80-year-old human's life, a million years for Sun would be about 3 days.

Maybe we're just in for some serious rearrangements as we adjust to a reduction in available resources, including the land we live upon. The great ocean currents could shift, altering climates and economies with them. Rising oceans and seismic activity could engulf islands and commerce-rich coastlines worldwide, altering the world's geography from New York to Bombay, from the Netherlands to Singapore. Changing global temperatures could destroy agricultural economies based upon monoculture practices. And we may not be ready for the day when we run out of oil—though the direct consequences of our profligate oil usage may pose a greater threat than the possibility of running out. Many believe that the Maya long ago predicted a major transformative change at the end of the present world age, calculated by them to occur on December 21, 2012. But nobody is quite sure of what form this transformation is likely to take.

Alternatively, we may be able to continue on our present path and eventually get to the point where Earth and its atmosphere are able to adjust to all our environmental destruction and learn how to cope with all of our pollutants and poisonous effluent. Microbes can be amazing machines, and maybe nanotechnology will develop nano-robots capable of neutralizing nuclear waste. And perhaps the United States, or the superpower that succeeds it, will eventually amass enough regulations, law-keepers, and weapons of mass destruction to enforce peace, happiness, and social order throughout the world. My last book sheds some light on the likelihood of this scenario ever taking place.

And of course, we may never know which of the above scenarios would have come to pass. Though we view ourselves as the primary beneficiary of life on this beautiful planet, we are alone in having developed the military capacity to swiftly destroy our own species and most of the other species on Earth. In the 30,000 or so years of human civilization on this planet, it is only in the past 60 years that we have acquired this chilling ability.

Since the end of the Cold War, the likelihood of blowing ourselves off the map in a multi-power nuclear conflict does look less likely. More likely would be another nuclear mishap anywhere in the world, such as that at Chernobyl, which is not checked in time. It was the heroic sacrifice by the fire fighters of Chernobyl that prevented an unstoppable meltdown situation from occurring. The reactor core would have then continued to spew intensive levels of radiation into the environment week after week, year after year—for thousands of years at least. Few of us ever consider what would have happened had the fire fighters failed, or not been willing to give up their lives in the effort. The consequences of that much radiation spewing into the global weather system on a continual basis are unthinkable, and the only ones doing the thinking thereafter might be a few of the hardier bacteria.

This isn't a very upbeat chapter, is it? Sorry about that, but we might as well acknowledge the possibly terminal implications of our civilization's current direction. It does not have to happen, and if I did believe that we were all irretrievably doomed then I'd have never bothered to write this book or my prior one, nor would I have bothered to dedicate many years to introducing natural and organic foods to the nation's diet, nor bothered to open a shop in order to introduce chaos theory, and its implications for society, to a wider non-scientific audience.

It has been a very full and busy life, always with the resolve to further and improve the evolution of our species on this planet. All of these activities have rewarded me with great personal happiness and satisfaction. My life has advanced from my activities in such a positive and joy-filled manner that I can only imagine that the invisible signs tell me I am not completely wasting my time—that it is not all too late. In the circumstances, it is no fun whatsoever being an old hippie saying "We told you so," but it must be pointed out that those who sought to fight for the environment and protest against its desecration were hounded, ridiculed and even jailed. Those who sought to live on the land with a zero carbon footprint were thrown off of it—and still are in most parts of the world. Laws have been enacted, now in force, making direct lobbying, protest and experimental lifestyles virtually illegal. Sometimes it seems like the ship is sinking and the response of those in authority is to ban the building of life rafts.

Let us hope that humans and their fabulous civilization are able by some means to steer a course through the major changes ahead. Let us hope we have not left it too late, when we eventually get around to it. If it is, then let us hope that by some means some members of our species survive whatever crisis we encounter and eventually re-discover how to live in harmony with the planet, and with ourselves. After all, we are special.

Human consciousness arose but a minute before midnight on the geological clock. Yet we mayflies try to bend an ancient world to our purposes, ignorant perhaps of the messages buried in its long history. Let us hope that we are still here in the early morning of our April day.
—**STEPHEN JAY GOULD** (1941-2002) AMERICAN PALEONTOLOGIST AND EVOLUTIONARY BIOLOGIST

Special people
us amazing newcomers

W HAT IS IT about being human that makes us feel so special? Only one key factor, our intelligence, seems to be more developed than that of most, maybe all other beings on the planet. Judged by almost any other scale of skills, we are regularly surpassed. We are physically weaker and more prone to disease than many other species. There are birds, fish, whales, turtles, trees, and fungi that are capable of outliving us, as well as humble bacteria. When we think of our eyesight, our hearing, or our sense of smell we can come up with many immediate examples of other animals that appear to out-perform us. Many other creatures enjoy skills such as radar and earthquake-detection that do not even figure in any comparison we would make.

We cannot even be sure that we are the most intelligent, since we have no way of assessing the intelligence of bigger-brained whales, 3,000 year-old trees, or the group intelligence of something like a giant underground fungus organism which may stretch for several kilometers and survive thousands of years. But we are very smart creatures and intelligence is a big feature of being human, compensating us well for most of our other deficiencies. We may not be able to smell as well as a lowly moth, see as sharply as a soaring eagle, or stomp as hard as an angry elephant, but we can develop machines that do.

Is our particular brand of consciousness a higher incarnation of the divine light of the cosmos than that of other species? Perhaps it is, and our higher level of intelligence is an indicator of just how much light we are capable of channelling, whether we choose to use the faculty or not.

We are special—can't you feel it? But can you accept as possible that otters and eagles, butterflies and cats, trees and dolphins all feel it too. Maybe mice and worms and sardines do not feel special, but for all we know they might be thinking the same thing about ticks and lice. But my interest is declared, I am a human and naturally biased. If any blue whales are reading this, then please forgive my arrogance in taking such a position.

So what is it that makes us so certain we are the pinnacle of evolution on planet Earth? Let us forget for a moment some of the depths of human depravity of which we are all well aware, and look at some of our uniqueness and beauty. Let us think of the things that we rarely, or never, see in other animal species and which we ourselves have developed to great heights. Yes, birds make music, but they do not write orchestral symphonies, nor have drums kits or keyboards. We weave never-ending diversity into music and song of all kinds.

Some animals, such as crows, develop simple tools, but none have ever developed the wheel, let alone the computer. Our tools evolve with the needs of our civilization and drive it along. Termites build a skyscraper that will be a home to many, and birds build homes designed to contain a single family. Neither of them have the understanding of architecture that would enable them to build both, as can humans. The difference between a termite mound and the Sydney Opera House, between the blackbird's song and a piano concerto, are more than just a difference of degree.

Alone in the natural world, humans dance wildly or in organized patterns, singly and in groups, to music. It sometimes seems so natural to be moving our bodies to music, yet there is no other species out there that has made this seemingly instinctive link between music and movement. Alone in the natural world, we do not just eat and forage, we have developed varied and highly developed cuisines, cooking with fire and preserving with salt and ice. The harnessing of fire made possible many of the qualities and skills separating us from the other animals on the planet.

As humans, we communicate subtly and directly, through many media, to other members of our species. We have developed drama and performance, portraying either life's real events or fantasies, which express emotions and convey ideas. We create and reproduce images on canvas, screen or paper in order to record and share memories of people, events in history, beautiful places and artistic visions. We have language, which enables us to express a wide variety of information, feelings and concepts—using any one of various media. And we have music. Most unusually, we have the ability to record, store and reproduce all of these forms of communication, whether print, audio or visual. Some of our written records go back several thousand years, some of those records describing events from even earlier times. We know something about our history.

We have groups, clubs and associations as a means for people to share ideas, make friends and manage common interests. We construct and live in houses of different shapes and sizes, from country cabins to towering skyscrapers, protecting our weak furless bodies from the elements. We specialize to a high degree in what we do with our lives—from baker to butcher to brain surgeon, from DJ to cab driver to Web designer. We have formed relationships with many other species of animals, domesticated them, and brought them into our care. Some we also eat. And of course, in relatively recent years we have developed technologies that would have been unthinkable to earlier generations, let alone any other species. Many of them have greatly advanced the enjoyment and fullness of life on Earth, as well as the dissemination of information and knowledge.

All of that is about what we do with our extra measure of intelligence, what we make of being human, and it does put us in a different class from all the other animals and species on Earth. But what are we—what is the essence of being human? We seem to have a unique interest in the meaning of life as well as the getting-on-with-and-enjoying bit of it. Do other species ponder the meaning of life and the purpose of the Universe? We have a rare curiosity that is sometimes content to seek without even knowing what is being sought. We find inspiration in different people and places, and spend time appreciating beauty for beauty's sake.

Are we better equipped to enjoy life than other beings, whether we actually manage to do so or not? Is our spirit able to carry on after death in a more coherent form than does the spirit of an old elephant, a cricket or an ancient tree? Are we cosmically something special?

That's another exciting thing about being human—however intelligent and knowledgeable we become, there will always be questions which we cannot answer and phenomena we cannot understand.

Acknowledgements

AFTER A FEW years of writing I thought that *Sun of gOd* (or *Perhaps...stuff is smarter than we think*, as it was then titled) was pretty much finished. Of course, it wasn't. Even though I knew what the book was about, it was by no means clear to anybody else. When I began sharing some of the concepts in the book with friends and strangers I further developed my own understanding while discovering techniques to make these concepts better understood by others.

Though I kept things close to my chest for the first few years, I had said enough to my old friend Arthur Edmund-Jones in Chiang Mai, at the end of 2000, for him to lend me an old guidebook he had to the world's major religions. It made me realize the need to address that whole arena. He and fiancée Pinit sorted me out for my month in Thailand, where I was undisturbed for the intensive first structuring of the book conceived at the start of that year. Hooking up with Claudia Boulton thereafter, on a trip in the Banteay Srei Temple in Angkor Wat, I remember first blurting out the full basic thrust of my book to somebody else.

There is always part of me that does not want my nearest and dearest to see early drafts (sorry to brother Craig and to others about this), since I particularly want them to read the final version, and with fresh eyes. Like myself, Craig has long been an intuitive devotee of Sun. But I gave early chapter drafts to my dear departed father, Ken, in case he would not survive to see that day. He loved everything he read, giving support from an important source.

I naively showed an early final draft to Jessica Woollard, a new friend and a literary agent. She made valuable and salient points that made me realize just how much work remained to be done. Then an author's Web site suggested that getting feedback from your friends is an effective way to do grassroots editing. I took their advice, sampling sections of the book and entire drafts to a selection of friends picked by an unknown process. They all helped and small comments sometimes made big impacts.

Emma then appeared in my life for a while. She had the irritating knack of radically re-arranging the paragraphs in a chapter I had carefully crafted—and improving it thereby. My old friend, David Style, read one of the earliest drafts, making supportive comments, and identifying a proliferation of commas. Ciaran Scott took a professional approach to the whole draft and prompted me to radically restructure the chapter sequence.

Freewheeling whale-saving Howie Cooke was the first of three houseguests whom I prevailed upon to read through the whole manuscript with a fine-tooth comb. I'd never realized he was an experienced proofreader, or that my book contained so many little discrepancies. Funny how a cool laid-back dude like Howie can be so anal about some things (thanks for every one of them, mate). My old girlfriend Charlotte got wind of what I was writing about and directed me to a few books that I needed to see, including Sir James Frazier's *The Golden Bough.* Soulmate Dinaz, who had told me about Zoroastrianism years earlier, dove through much of it and put me right on a few things, as she is wont to do. Astrological Laura saw some and has since fed me interesting solar links. Liza and Miranda both devoured manuscript sections and gave good feedback. Per and Aki barely dipped into it, but commented on the long paragraphs, and rightly so. My wonderful goddaughter Nicola helped me when I took the laptop on several of our travels and adventures. She made me realize the need for more clarity.

My old friend John "Hoppy" Hopkins read through the whole manuscript and I discovered that before leaping into the crucible of psychedelic

Sixties London, he had been a nuclear scientist at the Atomic Energy Research Establishment in Harwell. He cleared up a few of my fuzzier scientific points. The serendipity of a broken leg on a skiing trip landed me with Caras as a houseguest in my spare wheelchair until he was fit to return to his upstairs flat. His wide and often arcane knowledge, built up over eighty years, was put to good use.

The final wrapping-up took place during a month in 2006-7 of dedicated work in Sri Lanka, where I was wonderfully looked after by dear friends Eduard and Annoushka Hempel. There I met fellow author Rory Spowers who was to help me with spiritual support and publishing advice (keep trying and be patient). The writing was nearly over now, but always subject to improvement. Read-throughs and honest feedback by Claudia (of Angkor Wat), Jay Nardone (funniest guy I know), Dimitri (what a beautiful man) and Daryl (scholar of Tibetan Buddhism and Aboriginal ways/crazy house-guest/brilliant masseur) all made valuable contributions to the final tuning. And whenever a fresh manuscript is printed, I am prompted to reread it as though through new eyes, which always brings good changes.

I was thrilled when noted author Graham Hancock wanted to read my manuscript and hugely encouraged by his enthusiastic response, saying he read it "enthralled" and describing it as "wonderful, clear-headed, thought-provoking material." Support like this really helps when you struggle to understand why your message is not already obvious to all. And he wrote me a foreword! Thanks for introducing us, Sean.

And thanks go to the musicians and dj's and Internet radio stations so often feeding the music into me as many of the ideas emerged, whether at home or far afield. Special thanks to Pogo, Tristan, Laughing Buddha, Gaudi, Raja Ram, Shpongle, Stella Nutella, Nova, Solar Quest, and Radio 365.

Whilst looking for another exhibitor at the London Book Fair, I stumbled into my agent Susan Mears, who immediately grasped the importance of the concept and found me a publisher in Weiser Books who felt the same way.

At this point I enlisted old school pal Mike Barley, now Professor of Artificial Intelligence at Auckland University, to put me in touch with a scientific editor, leading me to Jason J, who clarified several areas and may have saved me from some embarrassment. Finally, I gave Craig a copy of the galley proofs to read, convinced this was the final product, and he managed to find a bundle of things that had somehow eluded all prior edits. Thanks, bro.

Like a ship on the ocean, I am supported by all those family, soulmates, friends and acquaintances who have given me love and helped me to just go on being me being different; supported by all those I have met and discussed deep ideas with throughout my life; supported by the synchronicity of the Universe. Thanks, thanks and thanks.

And final thanks go to that most special character Sun, whose rays I have so often savored, absorbing its energies whilst both enjoying and considering the wonder of its existence and ours.

Notes

1 The Big Bang is the most popular but not the only scientific theory of how this Universe formed. Well-accepted scientific theories are not infrequently revised or overturned by new evidence.

2 That would be from 200-400 million years real time.

3 This attitude dates back to Descartes, who convinced right-thinking people of the 17th century that a dog, being devoid of consciousness, is unable to feel suffering or pain. He nailed his own pet dog to the door in order to show how firmly he believed its yelps and cries to be unfeeling mechanical reactions.

4 *http://www.spirithome.com/spirpers.html#whois*

5 Cheaper than government ministers and probably less destructive to the system being managed.

6 The earlier Egyptian, Chinese and Indian cosmologies do not appear to have been subject to this misconception.

7 As are managing fire, standing upright, using complex tools, shunning nudity, and having a written language.

8 Mohammed consummated his marriage to child bride Aisha when she was 9 years old, and he 54. He also kept slaves, giving advice on how a good Muslim treats them. Some revered British and American historical figures also kept slaves and married girls well under 16.

9 "They shall beat their swords into ploughshares, and their spears into pruning-hooks; nation shall not lift up sword against nation, neither shall they learn war any more." —*Old Testament Bible*, Isaiah ii

10 Funny how they never teach about this stuff but never stop reminding us of those heroic early martyrs who ended up as cat food in the Roman Coliseum.

11 In some traditional tribal cultures, and in Iceland, such entities still retain a place in the culture.

12 By numbers of atoms, it's 90 percent hydrogen and 10 percent helium.

13 Degrees in the Kelvin scale are the same as Centigrade, but it starts 273 degrees lower, at absolute zero. Water freezes at 273 K, and 0 C. So subtracting 273 from any Kelvin number gives the Centigrade equivalent. Iron boils at 3134 K (that's 3407 C).

14 The author looks forward to the time when such use of the USA as a touchstone for extreme energy consumption may be obsolete.

15 Properly expressed, Uranus' axis is parallel to the ecliptic.

16 It is often apparent, from the roundness of astronomical numbers, that there is considerable uncertainty over actual distance, size, etc.

17 The other three are gravity, the weak nuclear force, and the strong nuclear force.

18 This was also approximately when the modern state was born, with one group of people controlling the activities of the rest, "officially" demanding sums of money or goods from them.

19 *Infinite Potential: The Life and Times of David Bohm,* by F. David Peat.

20 Sodium is a metal so unstable that it bursts into flames on contact with water.

21 E is in joules, M in kilos, and c² is 90,000,000,000,000,000, which is thousands of times more than Bill Gates is worth, counted in cents.

22 In fact, less than 1 percent of the uranium's mass is converted to energy during the nuclear reaction.

23 French biologist Jean-Baptiste Lamarck proposed that an organism is able to pass on to future generations traits acquired during its lifetime.

24 The other three are archaea, fungi, and protists. Archaea are very like bacteria but have a few different traits. Protists include protozoa, algae, amoebas, and slime mold. Fungi include yeasts and the organizations of cells that occasionally form into the surface organisms we call mushrooms.

25 Cirrus, cirrostratus, altocumulus, altostratus, nimbostratus, stratocumulus, cumulus, cumulonimbus, mammatus, billow clouds, and so on.

About the author

ENCOURAGED BY his father to "never follow the beaten track," Gregory Sams found himself at the University of California, Berkeley, in 1966 during the free speech protests and build-up to the Summer of Love. Sams' formal education ended with a fall from a tree on New Year's Eve at age 18.

Though he never got back to organized education, Sams' penchant for staying open to what's "out there" led to his role of introducing natural and organic foods into the British diet. He opened and ran Seed Restaurant, watering hole to the Sixties hippie community (including John and Yoko), started the UK's first natural food outlet, and later teamed up with brother Craig to develop Harmony/Whole Earth Foods, the nation's first importer/wholesaler of natural and organic foodstuffs.

Sams also published *Harmony Magazine*, to which John Lennon dedicated a cartoon, and *Seed: The Journal of Organic Living*, at a time when the concept of organic food was virtually unknown. From "watering the first shoots of green consumer consciousness," Sams went on to formulate, produce, trademark and promote the original VegeBurger, selling 250,000 burgers a week by the time he sold the company at the age of 39.

When Sams came across the chaos theory, he made it his mission to make the concept public. For him, the implications of knowing that throughout the Universe, things appear to be self-organizing along similar principles, should not be confined to the academic world. He opened Strange Attractions, the only shop ever dedicated to the chaos theory, and began creating original fractal designs and digital art for the company's posters, T-shirts and jigsaw puzzles, later successfully licensing these designs to others. Through the Science Photo Library, his fractal images have been reproduced by the millions in major magazines, newspapers and books, including on the cover of Fritjof Capra's *The Web of Life*.

Sams's first book, *Uncommon Sense–the State is Out of Date*, published in 1998, is an exploration of the lessons to be learned from chaos theory for how to govern our society through allowing it to create its own order. The book is available along with a gallery of fractal images at his website, *www.chaos-work.com*. He lives in London.

To Our Readers

WEISER BOOKS, an imprint of Red Wheel/Weiser, publishes books across the entire spectrum of occult and esoteric subjects. Our mission is to publish quality books that will make a difference in people's lives without advocating any one particular path or field of study. We value the integrity, originality, and depth of knowledge of our authors.

Our readers are our most important resource, and we appreciate your input, suggestions, and ideas about what you would like to see published. Please feel free to contact us, to request our latest book catalog, or to be added to our mailing list.

Red Wheel/Weiser, LLC
500 Third Street, Suite 230
San Francisco, CA 94107
www.redwheelweiser.com